Mud, Sweat, and Gears

Mud, Sweat, and Gears

A Rowdy Family Bike Adventure Across Canada on Seven Wheels

Joe "Metal Cowboy" Kurmaskie

With footnotes by Beth Biagini Kurmaskie

BREAKAWAY BOOKS
HALCOTTSVILLE, NEW YORK
2009

Mud, Sweat, and Gears: A Rowdy Family Bike Adventure Across Canada on Seven Wheels

Copyright by Joe Kurmaskie 2009

ISBN: 978-1-891369-85-8
Library of Congress Control Number: 2009940010

Published by Breakaway Books
P.O. Box 24
Halcottsville, NY 12438-0024
www.breakawaybooks.com

10 9 8 7 6 5 4 3 2

For Beth, Claire, Nancy, Ericka

Mothers and wives are the glue that holds the world together.

Contents

Prologue 9

Mom 15

Part One: Obed Summit

    Chapter 1 Second Wind 18

Part Two: Portland, Oregon, to Port Hardy, Vancouver Island

    Mom 27

    Chapter 2 How to Make the Perfect Cup of Coffee 31

    Chapter 3 Road-Testing a Perfectly Good Marriage 36

    Chapter 4 False Starts 40

    Chapter 5 Canadian Hospitality 52

    Chapter 6 A Brand-New Day 56

    Chapter 7 Little Russia 60

    Chapter 8 Ruckle Park: Fellowship of the Fire Ring 69

    Chapter 9 The Battery King of British Columbia 78

    Chapter 10 James and His Giant Peach Bicycle 83

    Chapter 11 Freefalling 94

    Chapter 12 Cross-Training 97

    Chapter 13 Haircut of the Gods 109

    Chapter 14 Grumpy Old Man, Part 1 115

    Chapter 15 Trying Not to Miss the Boat 121

Part Three:

Joe and Beth: The Greatest Love Story Ever Told (This Week)

    Mom 128

    Chapter 16 A Beautiful Wreck 129

    Chapter 17 Crash and Burn 154

    Chapter 18 As You Wish 161

Part 4: Prince Rupert to Saskatoon

Mom 176

Chapter 19 Selwin Berries 180

Chapter 20 Wilderness Gourmet 184

Chapter 21 Wendy and Her Lost Boys 211

Chapter 22 It's Best You Don't Know About These Things 233

Chapter 23 Yellowhead Highway Trivia for a Hundred, Alex
240

Chapter 24 Climate-Controlled Living 244

Chapter 25 The Gatekeepers of Jasper Park 247

Chapter 26 Jasper Welcoming Committee 251

Chapter 27 Grumpy Old Man, Part 2 254

Chapter 28 Gone to the Dogs 263

Chapter 29 Trucker's Dream 271

Chapter 30 Hailstorms Are All We Know of Heaven 277

Chapter 31 I Will Miss This Body So Much When It's Gone
282

Part Five: Nova Scotia

Mom 287

Chapter 32 Performance Art 291

Chapter 33 It's for You 297

Chapter 34 The Victory Tuck 300

Prologue

Life is a tragedy when seen in close up, but a comedy when viewed in long shot. —Charlie Chaplin

This is the love story I promised I'd never write. Granted, I made that vow at seventeen, packed to the gills with testosterone, Mountain Dew, and utilitarian philosophy: Rand, Marx, Nietzsche, the feel-good stuff. Those Danielle Steel novels—thumbed through on a sailing trip to the Dry Tortugas—were nothing more than poorly written, sexually absurd detours. In my defense, the only other reading material for fifty nautical miles were books on knots and outboard engine repair.

Love stories, in my cocksure teenage estimation, were for bored housewives and anyone who thought Air Supply was robbed of multiple Grammies.[1]

This was before life's hard bits. Before I learned that an honest love story is a disorienting mix of carefree summer evenings at the state fair and blood splattered across the highway . . . yours, mine, people we didn't know. People who might have become friends.

That idyllic Norman Rockwell portrait of the family at Thanksgiving dinner? See them sitting together, smiling as drumsticks and

---

1. Thank God we both hate bubblegum pop. I couldn't stay married to a man who rushed in banging his chest singing "Love Will Go On" while clutching a pair of Céline Dion tickets. Unless it was for a laugh.

mashed potatoes loop around the big table? Now put them in a flat-out sprint on some far-flung embassy roof, sound of gunfire in the distance, trying not to let hands slip from grasps as they fight smoke, fear, exhaustion, and chaos to chance the last flight out.

Everything that happens between the dinner table and the roof, there's your love story.

While no one will mistake my family for a Rockwell painting, and we've always maintained a strict No Air Supply listening policy, this, as honestly as we can tell it, is what happened to us between the table and the roof . . .[2]

Since we're on the subject of love, there has been competition—a real triangle to be honest. I fell early and hard. Over the years it's been quite a balancing act. It might have been easier on Beth if it were another woman. But how does one compete with steel, aluminum, and carbon fiber, the need for speed, and the call of the open road? I always wanted her to fall for the bicycle, too, but all those ads on Craigslist for "used once" tandems just prove that you can't force these things.[3]

2. While we're on the topic of honesty, I wouldn't be surprised if Joe tries to put some words in my mouth. We're supposed to be doing this footnote project evenings after I've been teaching high school. I know, originally he thought he was going to scam me into writing half his book through "she said" chapters. It gets late and I doze off while he's still reading to me. When I come to he's still typing like a madman over there. So honey, I don't want you making up a bunch of my footnotes, because, you know I love you, but I will cut you.

3. What's this? I've been nothing but supportive of his wanderlust and delusions he's living inside the movie *Breaking Away*. Besides, he hikes with me as much as if not more than he cycles. And then he sits at the computer for long stretches of time but never gets fat or out of shape. For years he's been claiming it's because he jiggles his feet all day long under the desk. I called it bullshit, but one day he comes to me with a peer-reviewed article about foot jiggling and weight loss. Thing about Joe, he's full of surprises. Maybe he wrote it himself under a fake name.

Of course Beth knows how to ride, but a nasty spill into a Santa Cruz roadway during college put her arm in a sling and off cycling, especially in traffic.[4]

It was only after my boys talked up our cross-country ride together that Beth warmed to the idea. For years I tried to lead her to the saddle by example when all I needed were a couple of pint-sized diplomats promising moose sightings, sun-drenched lakes, and weeks of unbroken family time.

When Beth came to me suggesting that she'd like to join our next project, a fully loaded family ride across Canada, it took some of the pressure off.[5] Partners in grime and all that. Still, I felt a little like the director of a film that was a lifetime in the making. I so wanted this to play big.

But saying and doing are two different animals. Canada would let the bike love in, build Beth's fast-twitch muscles, and open her eyes to all that could be learned in the saddle . . . or there would be one more Craigslist ad for a used tandem.

---

4. Jesus, that hurt, but it wasn't just my arm, it was my ribs, too. It did make an impression and could be what kept me off the bike for so long. Or maybe someone had to watch the kids before Joe started taking them with him.

5. I wanted to give it a go. Plus, my boys needed a proper adult along this time.

PART ONE

Obed Summit

Mom

Life's a pie fight, then you die.
—Fatty Arbuckle

Time to find out what the hell all this kicking's about.

Mom pinned up her Doris Day hair, pulled on her favorite Ann-Margret boots—the knee-high red ones, made specifically for walking—and waddled off to the doctor.

"With his sister, I felt a couple of nudges, the occasional kick on casserole night, but I could always calm her down with a scoop of rum raisin. This . . ." She pointed at her belly, which was roiling like an angry sea. ". . . is excessive."

The only time I quieted down was in the mornings. Mom, completely wiped out from another sleepless night, had to take care of a toddler, so she couldn't take advantage of this.

During episodes of The Twilight Zone *and certain acts on* Ed Sullivan *I also went still, confirming my affinity for twisted themes of social significance and American rockabilly music.*

That she'd let it go so long could only be attributed to the times she was living through. In 1965 pediatricians still smoked in front of their patients, told expectant mothers to enjoy cocktails as long as they weren't falling off the bar stool, and labeled anyone asking questions—beyond which brand of formula to use—a troublemaker.

Only the sustained ass kicking I was giving her could have sent my mother to that casual god's waiting room.

"Describe the pain for me."

She'd promised herself she wouldn't cry.

"Ever been in a prizefight with a kangaroo? Like that, except no one feels like ringing the bell."

She started to cry.

The doctor nodded during the examination, issued a few paternal smiles before the X-ray, let the nurse locate Mom a tissue, then sent her home to tough out the last trimester.

"Your baby is fine. Trying sipping some dark beer in the afternoons."

Mom sought some comfort by looking over the bloated belly that was me, to her stylish, red boots.[6]

"I don't drink," she whispered.

More kicking. This time hard enough for everyone in the waiting room to make out shapes against her belly. Mom swore loud and long, putting together combos to make the roughneck Spanish kids she once taught in Harlem proud. She thought of herself as a good Catholic, but Jesus H. Christ, enough was just about enough.

The other expectant mothers pretended not to notice.

---

6. Claire still loves her shoes. She has a closet full of them but her arthritis has forced her to wear tennis shoes most of the time. Every time she goes to put on Nikes she points at a picture on the wall. "I used to be able to stand on my toes for hours, in ballerina slippers. Joe's grandma lived to be 104. Don't let that happen to me."

The nurse offered a sympathetic smile. "Looks like this one's going to hit the ground running."

They had no idea.[7]

---

7. Claire talks a lot of nonsense but I believe this really happened. Joe's energy is daunting at times; he knows it and tries to play by the rules, but it's hard. He even refers to himself as a "chipmunk on speed" at times. But when he tones it down too much something gets lost. Pulling three kids across Canada seemed to equal things out, but even then maybe he was meant to live in a place with more gravity. Jupiter has a lot of gravity.

Chapter 1

Second Wind

If you let me run like the horses on the range, I'll never, ever complain.
—Timmy Curran, "Horses on the Range"

We were, by my best guess, three—maybe four—hard-boiled eggs from
Obed Summit, the highest point along Canada's Yellowhead Highway.

"Egg!" I yelled as I labored against our massive bike train; sixteen
feet worth of tandem, Trail-A-Bike, and trailer that made up, with
gear and my three sons, a gross weight somewhere near five hundred

pounds.[8]

Quinn, my nine-year-old stoker, began shelling another egg by repeatedly smacking it against his bike helmet, an artistic combination of force and finesse. From the seat of the Trail-A-Bike behind him, his younger brother Enzo stretched forward and salted my unlikely energy snack. These portable protein bombs made their way to the front of the vessel; sometimes whole, more often missing a few mouthfuls as the boys took a delivery toll[9]—supplementing the chocolate milk that served as their primary fuel—but this time I prayed for an intact shot of energy. We were going to need everything we had to top the summit.

Though a typical day saw us on and off the rig a dozen times before noon—for plastic lightsaber sword fights, swimming holes, and moose sightings—since sunrise, we hadn't broken our cadence once. It helped that one-year-old Matteo had buried himself in the caboose, sleeping off a full night of, well, sleeping.

Beth, on the single touring bike I'd loaned her, had replaced her usual back-and-forth riding pattern with a resolute pace off our rear.[10] The ramshackle carnival of conversations we'd been enjoying across Canada dropped off to a word or two; necessary commands only, sometimes a grunt of encouragement. When Enzo would point out a hawk standing on a fence post or a circling eagle, heads turned in unison for an appreciative look, exhaled a few "ahs," then went back to pedaling.

By perfecting this symphony of egg, chocolate milk, and muscle, we'd managed to best some substantial climbs. While I was proud as

8. It was something. Every time he got back on it and set it rolling I shook my head.
9. No one shelled my eggs for me.
10. Usual weaving back and forth? I might have been slower, but I learned how to hold a line.

hell of my pint-sized stokers, in comparison with Obed these were bumps in the landscape. I treated the preliminary ascents and infrequent flats like test runs, working the gears to find the ratio that would ring true to my legs once our final share of free momentum off the rollers ran out.[11]

"Here it comes, boys!" I said, gearing down as the cruelest bit of the Canadian Rockies rose in front of our wheel. Either I dialed in the sweet spot before gravity pushed down on us or it would break my spirit, slow the climb, and make everyone aboard pay.

I wanted my sons to understand that I needed them as I'd never needed them before, that I had to believe without hesitation in their youth, in the supple young hearts crashing around in their chests, in the power of their fresh, lean legs.

Instead I shouted, "All the Jack Johnson songs in the world won't save us now!"

The boys didn't have a clue what I meant.

Neither did I.

I actually started to come out of the saddle—my second-rate racer's body forgetting for an instant that it was not heading up a peloton but a mule train, hauling half of America behind it—then told myself to sit down and do the time, to work with the equipment instead of against it. I wasn't on a lighter-than-air, blessed-by-the-pope, high-performance bike that would leap into action the moment I stood up and hammered it hard enough. An out-of-the-saddle sprint would not only sap me but also probably snap a chain, and maybe fold our whole contraption in on itself.

I sat in for the assault on that jagged bit of landscape, looking right into the teeth of it, and knew I was in for a fight.

Obed has no switchbacks. It's a straight climb to a false summit—enough plateau to consider one's cursed existence—then on to another slope where the real work begins. I was busy marrying the pain and focusing on a spot two feet off my front wheel when I heard Beth's voice.

"Mush!"

She'd dropped in close behind the trailer and, like a seasoned coxswain for rowers on a faltering crew, was barking commands timed to help us find our pace.[12]

In the face of such stark grit and stamina—this trip was way over Beth's head—I had a moment's guilt that, the night before, after she'd drifted off to sleep, I'd handicapped her by shifting some of my heaviest payload into her four expedition panniers.[13] Loaded them to capacity and kept trying to jam in more. I quickly shook the feeling off, because if we were going to summit without stopping or, God help us, walking, I needed my full concentration (and while I will tell the world it's because I can only do so much, the darker truth is that I'm a shameful little man who, in my secret heart, always wants to crest first).

"Mush!" she barked. "Mush!"

We began to slip into a solid rhythm.

"Mush," she cried.

"Mellow!" the boys shouted, seeming to argue for a slower pace, which made no sense to me, but I was beyond caring. All that mattered was our forward progress. Beth's cheerleading was finding its way

11. I was always realizing I was in the wrong gear after it was too late.
12. Closest I'll ever get to doing the Iditarod.
13. Hey now. This is the first I'm hearing about this.

to my legs.

"Mush!"

"Room!" the boys yelled back.

Ah.

I located my groove and locked on to it. And on that trippy mantra our pace quickened and smoothed until—rare in life, and even more elusive in the saddle—we somehow found that moment when a group, be it paceline, peloton, breakaway, or family bike tour, morphs from mere teamwork into a single effort. For a few golden miles, it felt as if a cord[14] were connecting us tighter than coiled steel; I howled with joy, Quinn whooped, Enzo rang his bell, and Beth laughed loose and un-bridled. Even Matteo was awake.

When the summit sign came into view I spat in the face of the ac-cumulated years of knowledge that makes up the fields of structural engineering and human performance, and stood straight up in an at-tempt to hammer everything that mattered to me, all my imagined burdens and actual blessings, up and over Obed. It was irresponsible, even derelict behavior. But later, Beth would say that when Quinn and Enzo stood up and slashed at the pedals behind me, she'd never felt so proud.[15]

On top, we produced no American flag, peace cranes, or colorful Tibetan cloth squares. Instead Beth checked the boys for hydration and hypothermia while in their father's care, and nursed the baby, all while passing out plastic lightsabers and PowerBars with her free hand. Like

14. I don't know about this golden cord crap, I'm sure by the next downhill they'd left me in the dust. But I do remember that moment. It was sweet while it lasted.
15. That was worth all the hills and headwinds put together.

dandelions, my towheaded sons spilled across the high-altitude field in Alberta. I watched them run free as I sucked air, doubled over my handlebars.

Beth took her helmet off. In my mind it happened in slow mo, that long hair spilling over her shoulders. She resembled an Amazon. Xena Warrior Cyclist as sponsored by River City Bicycles; lycra instead of leather, Brooks saddle in lieu of riding bareback on a regal white horse into war and eternal glory.[16, 17]

"This the worst Canada can throw at us?" she asked. We both knew

16. Oh come on now. Joe's just hoping to get lucky again.
17. While that might be true it does not change the facts. —Joe

the answer, but laughed it off anyway. We could do so because Beth had become an entirely new creature from the one who had weaved across the border a month earlier.

No one could have predicted such triumphs when we wobbled out of the driveway of our Portland, Oregon, home for a summerlong unsupported bike trip around Canada. Rumor had it a few cynical neighbors were taking bets on a quick return and slightly slower divorce—I don't know if there were injury and demise brackets—perhaps the whole block was in on it.

The simplicity of our plan should have swayed them: a supported shakedown cruise from our front door to the Washington Ferry—to work out any kinks—then jettison the vehicle support and ride that mule train as far as we could before snow chased us home. We'd cover about seventy-five miles per day, camping about 75 percent of the time. To get back, we'd hop an East Coast flight before the autumn leaves lost the last of their brilliance.

This was not wholly unfamiliar territory, at least for me. With 140,000 miles of bike travel banked, it's something of a calling. I've crossed the length of the Australian Outback, half a dozen African nations, been all around America (once even towing Quinn, Enzo, and Dad's ashes), rolled through South America on road bike tires, rudimentary Spanish skills, and not a lick of Portuguese, even plumbed the depths of Copper Canyon, Mexico, one winter by mountain bike.

But Beth is one of those people who can't decide whether lycra's a conspiracy specifically against women, or designed to make everyone look this bad, who'd happily ride a single speed not to be hip, but to avoid learning how to use a shifter. The roadie rebel without a clue asking, "Take the lane? *Take the lane?* Which f-ing lane?"[18] Add to that a son celebrating his first birthday, plus the unpredictability of traveling with kids of any age, and I knew this could well turn out to be the most arduous adventure of my life.

Still, we had our reasons—good ones—to tempt fate. We'd always agreed that we didn't want our kids to become the kind of disaffected types who grow up trapped in climate-controlled, overscheduled, hermetically sealed childhoods—suffering Xbox carpal tunnel and nature deficit disorder. They'd tasted bike touring freedom and now had Beth convinced she didn't know what she was missing. I guess she figured it was time to put up or shut up.

My excuse is that I'm restless and unpredictable on foot, spastic and unwieldy even—but atop a bike, I'm poetry in motion. My pedestrian life feels like trying to jam Joey Ramone into a folk song. I fit into the world better on a bicycle.

I'll always want to go fast on two wheels, but these days the simple act of spinning pedals makes me whole. Any ride at any time helps keep my promises. Now that we had Beth halfway on board, all I had to do was deliver on those promises—of fresh roadside fruit dripping down chins and full days of sunshine stretched around spring-fed lakes, that we'd for sure see an actual moose and the largest mall on earth (marauding moose inside the largest mall would tie the whole room together for me). And that I'd somehow keep them safe through one hell of an adventure.

18. You have to wear lycra over the long haul to understand it. I still don't like taking the lane.

PART TWO

Portland, Oregon, to Port Hardy, Vancouver Island

Mom

She dropped her bags at the front door, then ran through the house calling our names. When Mom flew by the Florida room—which we'd converted into a gym the previous summer—she looked like a flamenco dancer. Dressed to the nines in a stunning outfit for her job as a Lancôme representative at an upscale department store, she fanned colorful tickets in both hands as she went.

We took a break between sets to find out what all the fuss was about.

"Get in the shower," she said, a little breathless. "I won tickets to the dinner theater production of Murder Most Foul. *But they're only good for tonight."*

My sister came into the room, applying makeup and slipping herself into a sundress I didn't know she had.

"Go," she instructed us. "Dad will be here in fifteen minutes."

This was big news. I had no feelings about the production, or what was on the menu, or that the whole thing would be hosted on a ship that might or might not sail while we enjoyed dinner and a show, but the importance of a teenage man-child getting to be that close to Valerie Bertinelli and the woman who had played Jane on Father Knows Best *cannot be overstated.*

"The captain of The Love Boat *is in the lead," Mom said, pushing us out of the Florida room.*

27

"Rick Springfield's the love interest," Jen said.

"Jesse's Girl," Tim noted, air-guitaring now.

Mom had been talking about the show for weeks. Rounding out the cast were Gary "Radar" Burghoff from M*A*S*H and the Professor from Gilligan's Island. It would be a greatest hits of our childhood TV viewing all on one stage.

Weeks before, Mom and Dad had engaged in a battle royale over getting tickets to this second-rate, celebrity-packed show. Dad ended it by saying he wouldn't spend that kind of dough even if the Love Boat *captain threw in a sailboat that he'd chartered from* Gilligan's Island.

So Mom's arrival with a handful of tickets on the final night of its run was the best kind of luck.

From the moment we stepped aboard until just before the closing act began, it was a perfect evening. Dad looked great in a suit from work. Mom had picked him one of the roses from our backyard garden that he tended himself. He wore it in his lapel.

Dinner was an all-you-can-eat buffet, which for two teenage weight lifters was a license to steal. And in what might have been a first I even thought about my outfit—a blue polo shirt, black jeans, and maroon cowboy boots—on the unlikely chance that we'd get to meet Valerie, or the daughter from Father Knows Best, *and one of them wanted to run off together.*

Dad leaned back, smiling and holding my mom's hand across the table. It was intermission, the desserts were arriving, and Gavin MacLeod was on stage, answering questions about what it had been like to be Captain Stubing.

He looked like he was in pain each time another question was asked, but then his million-dollar smile would return.

Mom leaned over, slipped some bills into my palm, and told me to get the waiter to bring Dad an extra drink and dessert "on the house" for winning the tickets.

Her wink told me everything I needed to know. She'd bought the tickets at work. The whole thing was smoke and mirrors and now I was in on it. I now knew Mr. MacLeod's pain.

Standing near the galley, waiting for the ship to sink or a waiter to come out so I could keep Mom's beautiful lie afloat, I had a moment of clarity. Valerie Bertinelli stepped out a door, crossed the hall, paused to mess with her famous hair, and in that instant turned and smiled. It was all I needed. I found a waiter, sold him on the lie, and went back to my seat.

It came off without a hitch—that is, until Dad asked the manager, coming by everyone's table to see if they were enjoying their evening, if it would be possible to meet the stars, since we were the special prizewinners of the evening.

It went to hell in a handbasket from there, the whole thing threatening to turn into a rotting pumpkin. We managed to hold it together in public, though the atmosphere at our table went from festive to funereal, that was until my mom turned and said, "Kids, every moment, we choose how to feel."

My dad chose to stew and sulk and leave his second dessert untouched, but the rest of us went back to clowning and having fun. Following Mom's lead, we gave Burghoff and the whole cast the standing ovation they clearly did not deserve. The rest of the room looked at us and began to stand.

As we were filing out, the manager tapped my father's shoulder. A quiet discussion followed, and we were led backstage. It was glorious, marred only by the fact that my youngest brother, Dan, got to sit in Bertinelli's lap for a photo, while I stood behind her with my hand as close as possible to her shoulder.

The manager gave my father a half-price coupon for the next production, starring Burt Reynolds and Jamie Farr. We were no-shows, but I learned important and dangerous things that evening. I learned that risk and caution battle in my DNA for supremacy—which has not made my life a cakewalk. But no matter what happens, I choose how to feel.

Chapter 2

How to Make the Perfect Cup of Coffee

Any real adventure begins and ends in the dark.
—Mark Jenkins

Following this maxim I got up the first morning in a campground outside Squim, Washington, stumbled around in the dark, and attempted
to brew the perfect cup of coffee for Beth. I'm strictly a sunsets-and-
tea man. Nonetheless, I adjusted my headlamp and focused on how

surprised Beth would be when I handed her a mug of gourmet java while pointing out the sun coloring the sky over the Strait of Juan de Fuca.

Since it was her first bicycle adventure of any magnitude, let alone one covering five Canadian provinces with three children in tow, I was pulling out all the stops. My strategy was that of any Zagat-starred restaurant: Make the coffee and the desserts irresistible and she'll keep coming back.

For a few seconds my headlamp spotlighted our triple-tandem Trail-A-Bike/trailer combo; eighteen feet of cycling train, a ridiculous marriage of engineering and necessity. What some had labeled "death trap," "monstrosity," and "divorce court on five wheels," I chose to see as a movable feast of fun, beauty, and no small measure of mid-life freedom. But I couldn't let its promises of family bliss distract me. Water boiled over on a WhisperLite stove. It was time to make the perfect cup of coffee . . . and my wife a believer.

Instead I knocked the pot off the camp stove with my knee. Time slowed just enough to contemplate the wisdom of buying a "new" set of cookware from a seconds clearance bin. Steam burns twice, but steam and boiling water soaking through fleece sweatpants will burn continuously—the same way Jiffy Pop popcorn scorches the kernels under all that space-age aluminum foil technology—until I realized that flapping around a picnic table, squawking obscenities like some injured ostrich with Tourette's syndrome, doesn't help.

Only pulling off one's pants does.[19]

19. Joe's answer to many of the mysteries in life.

Beth emerged from the tent to find me in pain and pantless, with steaming coffee-soaked sweatpants around my ankles, sunrise illuminating my inflamed thighs, arms fully extended, resembling a cartoonish version of Rio de Janeiro's Christ the Redeemer statue, complete with headlamp halo, the offending pot in my right hand, the lid in my left.

I respected Beth's confusion.[20]

"Typical start?" she asked.

"Pretty much," I said. After dressing the wound and redressing myself I took a seat in the dirt beside her. Disheveled, exhausted, in my element.

"Sometimes there's oatmeal, too."

I took a closer look at the burn.

"Coffee water . . . mishap," I managed, biting down on the words through a haze of hot poker pain. As if three words could adequately cover what she'd awakened to. The burn on my left thigh was already blistering into roughly the shape of Australia. Even touching the edges of the continent's territorial waters made me wince.

"You think I'll need medical attention?"

Beth squinted at my leg but looked like she might go back to sleep if someone didn't get her some java soon.

"Maybe just a few more damp baby wipes," I said.

Beth eyed the path of bumbling self-destruction to where I'd been standing when she emerged from her tent. Surely wondering if her hus-

---

20. You have to understand, Joe's unpredictability is his . . . trump card, or I guess you could call it strength. It would be his superpower really—that, and talking. But even for Joe, what I saw when I looked out of the tent was out of hand.

band could be the same man whom people sought out for athletic-related advice.

After all these years, I knew what else she was thinking. Torn between concern for my health and that pressing need for first-light caffeine.[21]

"I'll start a new pot," I said. "Soon as my leg finishes cooking."

Beth patted my head and put the water on herself.

She returned with baby wipes soaked in cold water. Her makeshift compresses felt like icy, backyard barbecue beer at a summer family reunion. A bit of Heaven with an aloe vera scent.

"How about that sunrise, eh?" she added. Either Beth was letting me save a few table scraps of dignity or she was perfecting her "ehs" before we crossed the border.

A new cup of coffee in her hand, we watched the first day of our adventure fill with light and expectations. The children weren't awake yet. It's when we do some of our best parenting.

This was the only real injury in four thousand miles. Most days I'm convinced I'm one of the last of my kind. The bicycle is my natural habitat, really an extension of myself, a better version of me. If I could do everything while on it I'd be tempted to try.

The burn started to throb more than it pulsed. I thought that was good. I chose to view it in those terms anyway. Beth handed me some more baby wipes.

"Your kindness is not lost on me, honey."

---

21. That is what I was thinking, and something to dip in it. That would have been nice, too.

Her smile wasn't quite right. A bit too large and satisfied. "Those are for the baby. Mr. Poopypants has a present for you in the tent."[22]

I wobbled to my feet. That was the pioneer spirit I'd been going on about. So rewarding that Beth was already embracing it . . . starting with a stoic attitude toward my injuries. Attagirl. I copped another handful of my baby's wipes, changed my own dressing, then limped over to the tent. Even our one-year-old would learn to sacrifice some possessions to make it in this outfit.

Lying beside my youngest son, I wasn't sure which of us was more helpless.[23]

22. Granted, Joe would end up carrying all the diapers and a lot more on his rig, but at the time he hadn't changed the little man in three days.
23. I was quite sure.

Chapter 3

Road-Testing a Perfectly Good Marriage

Buy the ticket. Take the ride.
—Hunter S. Thompson

Any marriage of length and substance is based on the fundamental principle of bait and switch.

No one sends themselves to the courtship front lines unless their plan is to grow old by the light of a TV screen and the mewing of too many shedding cats. What they do is recruit the best representation of themselves to charm and dazzle, form alliances and lasting accords with friends and family members, seed the emotional landscape with compliments, and offer up a generosity of wallet and spirit, paving the way to a free-trade zone of life stories, pheromones, fluids, and baby production.

If only that representative were a lifelong appointment. But the day comes when we must switch places with our more diplomatic selves, banish them to another dimension, to do charity work in Calcutta, maybe. Only to return some weekends, birthdays, and when the neighbors come over for dinner. This exile is not a malicious act; it's sheer exhaustion rather than a defect of character.[24]

Now if that "Up With People," Mary Kay Rep of you—a perky self-deprecating, *Parade*-magazine-scripted fraud—is still around and chipper a year into the marriage, your union doesn't stand a chance.

Like hell you say? Won't happen to us. We still shut the bathroom doors around here. This means you've never been introduced to the person rocking mindlessly in front of an open fridge wearing your favorite socks and polishing off the last of the good ice cream. You need to meet that piece of work, see if you can stand them after a knock-down drag-out, say-all-manner-of-crazy-shit-you-can't-take-back argument. It's the only way to know who you'll be sleeping with for the next fifty years. It's when the whole thing really gets off the ground.

Think of courtship as a quiet café in France. See how the late-afternoon sun lights her face, that perfect cup of coffee lies against his lips, and perhaps some hard bread and soft cheese is plated on the table between them . . . lovely.

24. People joke about the gap in ages: Quinn and Enzo are two years apart, then Matteo came six years later. I tell 'em we had to decide if we still liked each other. Closer to the truth is that we were so busy trying to corral two small boys that when we looked up, five years had disappeared.

Jump-cut fifteen years, to where even the best marriage will, at times, resemble weary refugees huddling under a bombed-out bridge in Kosovo. Notice them flinch at any noise, duck and weave through the chaos of their waking hours. That squinting is not the Paris sun in their faces, but the bowel-clenching torture of random bathroom schedules, the jolt of in-laws popping through for a visit, and unpaid bills that have fallen behind the couch.[25]

Each day ends with a serpentine dash to the covers and dreams of the next patch of safe haven; a matinee movie on a Tuesday afternoon, alone, or the rare dinner for two when the kids are off at sleepovers.

Any relatively unmediated couple know they've been sold a bill of goods. Those who accept delivery are drawn to the theater of the absurd and will, statistically, outlive their single counterparts. I'm convinced this is due not only to advances in medicine, but to the need to see what crooked path of hooligan mischief the other will lead them down next.[26]

Val-da-ree, val-da-rah, val-da-rah-ah-ah-ah!

These are the good marriages, mind you. And ours, I believe, is better than most. There's real laughter, sometimes while crouching under that bombed-out bridge, even. We've squirreled away some hard

25. They fall behind the sideboard.
26. There's been plenty of hooligan mischief, believe me. With three boys, four counting Joe, I'm outgunned and outnumbered. Even our cat is a boy. Joe brought home an ant farm one time, Uncle Milton's, and I'm reading the instructions. The ants are all boys. I can't get a little estrogen into the mix for love or money. With the ant farm, Joe couldn't get those buggers to go into their plastic home. Some of them got out and ran wild over the breakfast table. He had to rig a straw up to the hole and vacuum the ants out of the travel tube, then blow them into the farm maze. The boys ran around like banshees, Joe sucking and blowing ants, some of them biting him and making a break for it, with the boys laughing and hooting. There's your hooligan mischief I live with every day.

bread and soft cheese in the unlikely event that the French café in the distance is not another mirage. When once upon a time we broke china in anger, frustration, or fatigue, it was more often the cheap plates, and even if an heirloom or two went down—so be it.

A certain amount of collateral damage should be expected when two souls try to invent themselves together. In our case, with one painful exception, it's been nothing more than sound and fury.

If a marriage is the invention of *us,* everyone involved should be willing to blow up the lab in the name of Science. Places people. Safety goggles. Something could go bang.[27]

---

27. As a high school chemistry teacher, I don't approve of this metaphor. The safety goggles, okay, but we don't need to blow things up all the time. What is it with boys?

Chapter 4

False Starts

All life is an experiment. The more experiments you make the better.

—Ralph Waldo Emerson

"Seeing as it's a bicycle trip, we should probably get on that behemoth for a shakedown run."

We were stretched out on lawn chairs (someone else's) near the water's edge. From there we could see Canada as clear as day. Technically though, it wasn't a Canadian bicycle adventure until we'd reached Her sovereign soil on two wheels.

I was loath to break up the boy's reindeer games, but we'd been in Squim, Washington, for two days, just a stone's throw from the Discovery Trail, a converted rail corridor that would take us right to the ferry.

Our kids made fast friends with a rowdy cabal of like-minded boys—all of whom bonded over lightsaber battles and amused themselves for hours by playing a seafaring game they called "You've Sunk My Crabbleship."

The rules: Catch a bunch of crabs. The ones who live through the ordeal are set afloat on large pieces of driftwood, launched from a floating dock. An arsenal of sticks and rocks have been stacked on this dock. Most of the crabs would need days to figure out how the hell they got onto the high seas, that it's not a pleasure cruise, that fighting their fellow crabs is fruitless, and that bailing into the water at any time would be an excellent idea. The ones who blindly stumble off the sides won't get to see the sky open up and rocks rain down. Fortunately, excitable young boys have terrible aim in the heat of the moment.

Watching them, I'm reminded to reread *Lord of the Flies* . . . for parenting tips. My boys' energy is constant and unquenchable. Children only get stronger as their parents fade and come undone. All part of God's cheeky little plan.

Their aim seemed to be getting better. Crabs were in real peril and there wasn't a boiling pot of water handy to help complete the circle of life or dinner.[28]

Time for a nice, long bike ride.

We parked the Subaru, unloaded all eighteen feet of contraption in five or six pieces, then rebuilt it on the side of the road. Panniers were added and we dressed ourselves in gloves and helmets, clipless shoes and matching River City Bicycle Shop jerseys; a family portrait fit for the cover of *Outside* magazine.[29]

"Okay, everyone, on three."

Follow your folly wherever it leads.

"Steady now."

Pursue it with the rabid ferocity of a mad dog or an Englishman left too long in the midday sun. Of course, you might end up a pile of bleached bones, a roadside caution sign for the rest of us to ponder through the remains of the day.

"Pedal hard, gang . . . harder!"

Rest assured though that your fate will not involve a slow-as-molasses fade, full of regrets while becoming one with the couch.

"Lean left. Damn it, your other lefts."

A bold statement, following one's folly. Purposeful and lively on paper, it's an entirely different animal for those who actually play it out.

28. I had suggested some rock and shell collecting along the shore, which lasted about ten minutes, until they found the crabs.
29. It was the last time those outfits would look magazine-cover-clean the rest of the tour.

"Watch the gravel!"

I've been accused of folly hunting from the saddle of a bicycle. While I can see how that impression's been fostered, what with my tendency to work a story into a frothy lather, my dirty little secret is that I've never actually redlined my life out of control.[30]

I'm more a cardboard cutout of an adventure traveler when set beside my ancestors. (*Rest stops? Convenience stores? Let me tell you something, it would be "convenient" if an animal wandered along so we could club it to death, eat for a week, and wear fur through the winter.*)

"Less pedaling!"

I've been spooked, a little hungry, tired, bitten, barked at, hit by the smallest car in Ireland (about the size of a refrigerator box), almost kissed the Blarney Stone (could have been fatal), but I've never been terrified on a molecular level . . . not yet. A darker patch of me wonders what the view's like from that side of the chasm. But I lack the proper-sized testicles, tattoos, or fiber in my diet. I haven't taken that walk on the wild side, not really.[31]

"Keep your hands on the bars. That means everyone!"

Until that afternoon on the Discovery Trail.

We were having a little trouble finding a rhythm. Truth was we were all over the trail. Not something I expected. When I'd thought how this family road trip would play on one very long bicycle, the soundtrack always featured something along the lines of "Bicycle Built for Two," not Ozzy's "Crazy Train." I imagined beaming faces, a tail-

---

30. Yes he has.
31. How many people do you know who have soloed across the Australian Outback by bike?

wind, and general adoration in my direction.

Over intense exertions and white-hot fear, I thought I heard some whimpering behind me.

Test-riding this behemoth back home may have been unwise with only balled-up newspapers jammed in the panniers. Still, we'd had a whole session, just the adults, on a quiet country road in Oregon's Willamette Valley wine country—to see if we could handle a triple tandem. It took a few tries, some tense moments, but we'd gotten it down, even laughing and congratulating ourselves in the sunshine. As we pedaled along, admiring the grapes, maybe both of us were thinking this was a snapshot of days to come.[32]

Weaving onto the Discovery Trail felt like we'd crossed a line. Had I really cheered Beth, my true companion, mother of our three sons, and long-suffering wife of my cycling antics these seventeen years, to hop on an untested bicycle train and see how far across Canada we could get before snow chased us home?

"Hang on." I braked harder than I wanted to but, through instinct and muscle memory, found the side of the road without putting it down.

Talk about laying my marriage on the line. In a world where most of the big animals that can paw your head off flatfooted have been hunted down or jailed for profit and viewing enjoyment, I'd pried a cage door of emotions open and let something big and unpredictable break free.

---

32. I remember thinking this is fun but what about the rest of the train? Shouldn't we try that out before retiring to the clubhouse? But Joe distracted me with dinner plans.

"Everyone upright?"

Nods, ashen faces.

One way or another we'd find out if this beast could be harnessed for the ride of our lives or carry us into the tall grass, away from everything we've cared about, never to be heard from again.[33]

"Let's take five."

Everyone was already getting off the bike anyway. We were quite a sight by the side of the road: the Swiss Family Robinson of Cyclists. But every picture tells so little of the real story. Even stripped down to bare necessities we weighed in at close to 450 pounds, not counting adults. Just to arrive at that hefty number I'd held a weight loss seminar in our driveway early one Sunday morning. The touring cyclist's equivalent of a holy roller weight loss tent revival. Come to Jesus and turn in your burdens. Also, Sunday mornings find my brood groggy and docile. I figured I could work them over while they didn't have all their wits.

Space was at a premium. But how to make this point without sounding cruel or fanatical? While I steeled myself for a protracted back-and-forth battle with the boys over everything from Pokémon cards in metal lunch boxes to every piece of sporting equipment known to man, my pint-sized posse folded like cheap card tables. I had only to remind them of all the hobo treasures, pool floaties, bats, and balls we'd picked up roadside on the previous cross-country ride.

Re-creating another scene out of *Lord of the Flies,* the boys instantly off-loaded excess baggage, and most of their clothing.[34]

33. I just wanted off.
34. I snuck a few of the boys' clothes back into the bottom of their bags without Joe noticing until it was too late.

It was Beth who stonewalled.

"The latest Harry Potter installment? In hardcover? It's nine hundred freakin' pages![35] Hasn't Ms. Rowling ever heard of a contraction? Wait, she's British, only the queen's proper English will do." I shook the massive tome, doing a pretty good imitation of Malfoy. "If I see it back in the pannier, I swear I'll read the ending out loud and ruin it for everyone." An obvious bluff, but I was still gobsmacked from the surreal clothing battle, which had featured a stack of cotton T-shirts and several pairs of jeans.

"Cotton kills," I'd announced, holding up an article of clothing that looked great on the rack at Urban Outfitters but was absurd on a bike trip.

35. I won the Harry Potter book battle by agreeing to carry it in my bag the whole trip. Then I traded it for the Canadian version with a wonder family on Salt Spring Island. Their copy, like everything in that country, is less showy and puffed-up than in America. The book was half the width and length and weighed maybe a third of our version. But it did have all the queen's proper English in it.

"Baby, wearing these cotton shirts is like rolling down the road wrapped in wet dishrags. They stay heavy and hold an amazing amount of stench for days."

Sticking her tongue out at me. This was Beth's entire rebuttal. Juvenile, but oddly effective.[36]

"Wash and wear, people. That's the drill." I palmed my entire wardrobe in one hand. "We bring lightweight, multipurpose outfits, wash one by whatever means necessary—mountain stream, rock, or garden hose—while wearing the other. If it doesn't dry from body heat and a bit of breeze, it stays home."

They resembled a classroom taking Italian for beginners. Nothing was getting through. I knew it sounded ridiculous to the uninitiated, but I was speaking gospel if we hoped to cross a healthy chunk of a continent by bicycle.

36. Try it. While it doesn't always work, it feels great. Like you're ten years old again.

"We're gonna wash clothes on rocks?" Quinn asked.

Beth shoved a pair of pants into my arms. "My cute jeans make me feel like a woman."

I held up the offending garment.

"These will puff up like a blowfish and weigh more than a meteor the first time they get wet."

Beth nodded. "Then we can't let them get wet. Store 'em with my coffee and guard 'em with your life."[37]

Back roadside, there was Gatorade in the water bottles and loose gravel under our front wheel, but no momentum. We tried again.

"Steady now, steady!"

Our train wobbled along for fifty yards, then we nearly tumbled. I stopped, cursed, regrouped, and wobbled some more. This process was repeated about five times back and forth over the same hundred yards near the Discovery Trail entrance.

"We're not getting very far," Enzo pointed out.

For variety, I'd trade cursing for pep talks, but the fear in Beth's voice kept stopping me in my tracks.[38]

Unlike previous delusions of grandeur that had worked out through a combination of denial and Forrest-Gump-sized naïveté, doing this on the triple made crossing the length of the Australian Outback solo seem like a pedal in the park (a sweltering park rife with

---

37. And in an unexpected side benefit, I got to smell my favorite roast every time I walked around in my cute jeans.

38. It was a nightmare. I really thought Joe was going to start crying from the frustration. He wanted to make it work so bad, but a blind man could see we were a no-go.

poisonous reptiles, devoid of moisture and good sense, but a park nonetheless). It dwarfed seven cycling adventures across America, even the one done while towing two young sons, my dad's ashes, thirteen feet of bicycle, and 250 pounds of gear. Rolling the length of South America on road bike tires, rudimentary Spanish skills, and not a lick of Portuguese? Chump change. I'd plumbed the depths of Copper Canyon by mountain bike during winter with only a light jacket. I'd even crossed five African countries with not a fence between myself and the wildlife . . . and only a bike for a weapon.

But ten minutes pedaling on Discovery Trail with all of us? Madness.[39]

I wasn't going to ask Beth to ride her own bicycle, though. I wouldn't hang her out to dry like that. Not on her first long-distance ride. A bulldog of a backpacker, a field biologist by profession, Beth knows her way around a campsite and thinks nothing of hiking for days on a trail. But her own bike? Out of the question. I winced recalling her testing the Terry seat as she pedaled aimlessly in the same gear. I'd asked her to do some miles on the wind trainer in our basement. Watching her fool around with her hair and play with the stereo remote while she pedaled, I was never happier knowing we'd all be joined at the hip.

It was always the plan to have her sitting behind me the whole way. No need to master the subtle art that is gear shifting the Canadian Rockies.

Best-laid plans . . .

While it's possible to pedal a triple bike long enough to qualify for

---

39. Thank God he admitted it right then. He'll try other crazy schemes in the future but it's good to know even he can see a limit.

a trucker's license, it's problematic. Picture a rolling Bowflex machine that tips from side to side without warning. Now put this unwieldy personal gym into traffic. It wasn't so much the length as the way it was configured. We really needed Beth in the third seat to balance the ride. It wasn't the right bike for the job.

Also, no matter what the official tourist brochures and state maps wanted you to believe, the Discovery Trail was not complete. Rather than meandering along a crushed-gravel rail-trail, we found our fish-tailing fitness center back on highways where we had to battle the hot breath of log trucks and dodge the bumpers of distracted tourists late for the ferry.

We took another five. I was sweating buckets by then, half out of exertion, while the other half was flop sweat, the kind felt by night terrors, stage fright, or the breaking of a bad fever. Beth looked pale and unhappy.

"You're the expert," she said. "If you think we can do it with this setup, I'll soldier on."

I looked her in the eye. "We could. I suppose we'd get better at it. But it's too white-knuckle to make a go like this."

"Thank you, Jesus." My wife did a little Homer Simpson victory dance. "When I wasn't terrified or flat-out panicked," she said, "I was a whirling dervish of fear."

Beth assumed we were homeward-bound. Her celebration was short-lived.

"New plan. You'll solo on my trusty touring bike. I'll convert the triple-coupler Santana into a bicycle built for two and muscle all three boys across Canada with you in front, or sometimes behind us."

She was stunned.[40]

"I'll keep you in our sights at all times," I said. We both knew this was a preposterous lie.

It wasn't what she'd signed on for. She'd need to keep up with the caravan under her own horsepower. Nothing if not a firebrand Italian, Beth didn't shoot the plan down outright.[41]

"On the bright side, I'll be burdened with a long-haul bike, three boys, and most of the baggage."

Beth wasn't buying it.

"Didn't seem to slow you down the last time," she said.

"I'm two years older, there's a lot more bike and, don't forget, an additional child." I attempted a pained expression.

God love her, my wife walked over to the front of the tandem.

"Just remind me how these gear-shifty things work again."[42]

---

40. I was relieved. No matter how hard it was to wrap my head around soloing across Canada. I would have taken a bullet before getting back on that beast.
41. What plan? Joe was just making it up as he went.
42. Even after I learned how to work the gears I still thought they were broken sometimes. Turned out it was just me.

Chapter 5

Canadian Hospitality

Kindness is always fashionable.
—Amelia E. Barr

Steve and Melissa were the perfect welcoming committee. The Canadian government would do well to put them on the payroll. A lively couple in Victoria, they were well within their rights to turn us away. Steve wasn't more than a few weeks out of prostate surgery, but still trying to build onto his house. And Mel was working full-time while helping Steve recover, i.e., not fall from a ladder or work himself into the grave.

We'd e-mailed them through Warm Showers, a listserv/club where cyclists provide accommodations for one another when on the road. I can't speak for the entire network, but we've had nothing but amazing experiences with the Warm Showers experiment. College students on their big road trip to find out what was beyond institutionalized education, seniors doing the world upright, a Japanese calligraphy artist who taught the boys how to write their names in Mandarin with quill pens and velvety black ink.

The parade of folks who have enjoyed our home has brought us more than we've given them. And after the life I've lived, it provides me a deep sense of return, giving back for all those years I was scooped up and offered a bed, food, and friendship.[43]

Since we'd had to do some quick transporting of a second bike for Beth, along with more panniers and gear, Steve and Mel stepped up again, agreeing to let us park a vehicle in their driveway. We'd pick it up on the return flight from Nova Scotia.

As we set up our tents in Steve and Mel's backyard, I met their neighbor Al. Or more accurately, he leaned over a wooden fence and, without proper greeting, handed me an apple and launched into his life story.

Al was standing in front of a lovingly restored 1965 Pontiac GTO. Steve told Al not to "bother" us, but he was clearly joking. You could

43. Joe's been bringing home cyclists our whole marriage. They were always fun if a bit smelly, but I worried at times that there might be an ax murderer in the bunch. Since taking the trip across Canada by bike, I better understand and appreciate what it all means. I ask Joe when the next cyclist will be stopping by.

tell they were close. Discovering Al was eighty-six years old was one of the greatest shocks of the entire trip. The man's hair was perfect, I mean Werewolves of London perfect.[44] And the way he dressed, Al could have passed for Tom Jones. I have never met an octogenarian before or since who still wore shirts open to the fourth button, gold chains, and stylish sunglasses, the type that didn't cover the entire square footage of his face like a blind barn owl. On anyone else this look would have been laughable, but Al pulled it off. He pumped me full of apples while regaling us with stories; in all of them he was a cross between Indiana Jones and Austin Powers. I doubted much of it was true, but I believed every word.

"My son's a lot like you," Al noted. "He goes for it every day."

Fathers should talk up their sons or daughters. I can't hang with a guy who would bad-mouth his kids or holds back affection because he thinks it's character-building.

The greatest joy a parent has, besides spending their lives with their children, is talking about them. What I did not expect was that Al would back up his son's achievements with a faded newspaper clipping extracted, on the spot, from his wallet.

"He played for the Red Sox," Al said.

The article was about a no-hitter he'd thrown back in the 1970s against Mr. October himself, Reggie Jackson. Al could recite the article verbatim, but as I read it, he added in his own flourishes and asides.

It endeared me to him even more.

Later, Steve said, "Believe me, Al's outfit isn't even a costume. You

---

44. It was a rug. Joe still hasn't figured that out.

should see the parade of women he's brought home in that GTO over the years. When he's not playing cards or running some deal, in the real world or his head."

Al had decided to live until he dropped. An expression he used earlier stayed with me: "There are plenty of ways to lose your life without dying."

I saw it too many times, every day.

"Al's gonna outlive us all," Steve noted.

In a way, he already had.

Chapter 6

A Brand-New Day

When you are through changing, you are through.
—Bruce Barton

Beth's metamorphosis, apparent in less than a week, was just this side of miraculous. With any miracle, things had to look hopeless for it to count for anything. That, timing, and context. Imagine if Jesus had turned water into wine coolers at an Applebee's on a Tuesday? It wouldn't have impressed the happy-hour crowd unless he'd worked the Buffalo wings into shrimp while he was at it.

But Beth, a nursing mother, on her first bike trip longer than twenty-five miles, had me in awe. Her maturation included several glorious trials by fire, a few of which looked more like crime scenes than character-building experiences.[45]

Her darkest hour was also her turning point. It came on the Galloping Goose rail-trail, a dream ride from Victoria to French Beach on the western end of Vancouver Island. People asked why we headed west on a bike trip to Nova Scotia, but easy grades, pristine camping, coastlines, and no cars allowed Beth a primer before hitting the open road.

Sometimes you have to head in the opposite direction to get where you want to go. And sometimes your life sounds like a fortune cookie, but it was working so I didn't monkey with it.

Seven days in on The Goose, as we'd begun to refer to it, Beth dropped off the radar. In my mind, anything might have happened. She'd already suffered a number of firsts: her first pedal gouge (that ankle only bled for a few miles and clotted up on its own) and, even more horrifying for her, the initial assault of a biker's tan. ("How am I going to look in a bikini now?")[46]

It took us a few miles to realize she was AWOL. In our defense, as soon as we noticed, we heeled our yacht around and set off at full steam on a search and rescue. We found her lying in the dirt beside the road,

45. I didn't know which way was up for the first few days. It was a blur of sore legs and sweat, but slowly I started to come around.
46. The answer: Swim in your bike shorts or sport your bike tan in a bikini with pride. Either way, it's about getting over yourself.

fixating on clouds, in a full-blown low-blood-sugar daze.[47]

Quinn and Enzo, having witnessed this behavior in their old man on previous rides, began reviving her with bagels and sweet and salty granola bars, adding extra cream cheese for good measure.

Beth's gaze was still slightly out of focus when she looked at me and said, "You bastard."[48]

I nodded uncertainly. In agreement with the facts, but unclear where they were leading.

"Lying here, I realized something."

This couldn't be good.

"I realized you rented our house for the summer."

She dusted herself off and accepted the handlebar—a promising sign—and said, "I couldn't go home if I wanted to." Then, with a dignity I could not attain were I to live longer than a hobbit, she patted the seat. Considering, perhaps for the first time, the true depth of hooligan mischief that knowing me had led to.[49]

She studied her Terry Butterfly seat, patted it once more, and said, "This is my home now."

We wanted to give her all the time she needed. Instead Beth clipped into her pedals, looked at us like we were slackers, and said, "Let's do this."

That wasn't the end of it . . . there were little dramas and occasional second thoughts, but it didn't take long for her to settle in with style. Laughing off rumors of cougars in the North Country, nursing our

47. I wasn't counting on anyone noticing my disappearance for many miles. What they didn't know is that I had to eat stale Cheerios out of the back pocket of my jersey to hang on.
48. That was letting him off easy.
49. Did he just call me a hobbit?

one-year-old between thunderstorms, swigging chocolate milk on the fly, swimming in cool lakes at lunch stops, offering a misplaced confidence in my ability to fix anything on the bicycles, taking detours of interest without thinking of the extra miles, and even taking the lane on narrow downhill runs.

"You make your past your past," we're always telling each other, and depending on the day or discussion, we even believe it.

"Do that again and I-will-cut-you." That's another one we're fond of.

When she entered a hotel pool in bike shorts and a sports bra, the transformation was complete.[50]

Salt Spring Island became her coronation. She geared through the steepest rollers when I had to admit defeat and walk the mule train, with all its burdens, up the last ten yards.[51] An amazed circle of tourists surrounded her on the top deck of the ferry. With baby Matteo strapped to her back, I heard Beth sharing the discovery that a bike's tempo allows for stops at every art studio, sustainable farm, and microbakery along the way.

"Even gluten-free pizza tastes incredible on a bike tour." Some of the women, about her age, were listening so intently you'd have thought it was an episode of Oprah.

"Food means so much more on tour," she announced one afternoon between bites of sun-dried tomato bruschetta.

"Everything means more on tour," Quinn added.

Enzo looked at us. "But I still don't like grapes."

50. When I arrived home from Nova Scotia and all my clothes were too big and I could see muscles in my legs I never knew I had, that's when the transformation was complete.
51. Yes!

Chapter 7

Little Russia

Although golf was originally restricted to wealthy, overweight Protestants, today it's open to anybody who owns hideous clothing.

—Dave Barry

"Man, I feel like one of you should be holding a school bus stop sign that flips out."[52] This from a pierced mouth of teenager on a BMX bike. He was the informal greeter of Sunny Beaches Campground. His shirt was a play on Nirvana's famous album cover *Nevermind,* but instead of the baby underwater taking its first dip, his had a BMX bike underwater floating in the same way. NEVERMIND THIS! the lettering across the bottom read. I decided it wasn't supposed to make sense, but it looked right on him.

Also, calling us a school bus of the bike world nailed it. I had half a mind to find a flip-out stop sign in a salvage yard and try to jury-rig it onto the handlebars.

Nevermind This! wheelied up closer to our mule train. He did little moves, lifting the back wheel up, twisting it around while he stood on posts that stuck out from the front wheel, all with a casual indifference that told us this was like breathing for him. Another moment to inspect our setup and think it over, then he was giving the boys high-fives.

"That has gotta be the raddest thing I've seen all summer."

He circled back around to me, extending a gloved hand into the air for me to smack. "Way to keep that shit real, old man." Emphasis on every word.

I rather liked his assessment, except for the *old man* part. Then he introduced his dad, who looked all of thirty, in the same fashion.

I felt better.

We were at the end of an extremely full day of exploring the Galloping Goose rail-trail. Serious consideration had been given to push-

---

52. It really did look like this, especially when he'd stop along the side of the road and I was behind him. The boys would pile off like it was a bus stop.

ing into the bonus part of the summer day—there's morning, after-noon, and the after-dinner light that hangs around until about ten o'clock during that time of year. We wanted to see if we could make Potholes Provincial Park. But it's what often lures a cyclist: This camp-ground was at the bottom of a long hill. There's even a term for a de-scent that comes so late in a day's ride: the victory tuck.[53] You get down in the crouch, feel the speed, and don't want to do anything but cross a line, throw your hands in the air, then look for the podium and the reporters.

No one had the heart, that early in our trip, to take on the next as-cent when a perfectly good spot—one advertising a pool and putt-putt golf—was another easy left turn and more victory tuck to the water's edge away.

Besides, Sunny Beaches . . . the name alone warmed the heart and put a bounce in one's step.

"The pool? Ah . . . right . . . it's covered in leaves and a thick layer of slime," Nevermind This! said. "Every summer we come back here, I wish they'd drain it so I could get some riding in, do verticals and grab air."

53. You know Joe make these phrases up, right? No one calls it a victory tuck . . . not yet. In his first book, *Metal Cowboy*, he coined the expression "cockroaching," mean-ing when you push yourself too hard on the first or any ride of the season or tour or world adventure or you haven't trained enough for a big race, ride cyclocross, or what-ever. You end up on your back by the side of the road, hands on your chest, spasming out the cramps in your feet by kicking them into the air. Years later we were watch-ing a leg of the Tour de France at the Lucky Lab Pub in Portland when Bob Rolle asked Lance about his hard-fought comeback on that day of the race. Lance looked right at the camera and said, "I'll tell you, Bob, I almost cockroached over the Pyrénées." The pub exploded with laughter and folks kept coming by to pat Joe on the back, shaking their heads. My husband had worked one of his expressions into the lexicon. Trust me, that meant more to my husband than anything this side of his family. So here's to the victory tuck. Use it with Joe's blessing.

The boys groaned about the pool.

"Brett's pretty good too," his dad said, tapping his boy's bike handlebars. "But he's hell on wheels when it comes to racing. We're headed for the BMX Invitational Series over in Victoria all weekend."

My sons perked up at the mention that Brett would get his ramps and rails out of the RV and do tricks for them after dinner.

"The putt-putt?" Brett kinda smirked at the mention of this amenity. "That's open for sure, little dudes, but I bet you'll never play a course anywhere like it in the world."

Brett's dad shook his head. "Damn Russkies who run this place, they just aren't right. I mean, they're all right, but they aren't right."

On that cryptic note, we rolled over to the store to register.

Ten minutes in the place and I knew what Brett's dad was talking about. By the way, they were Polish, not Russian, which wasn't here or there when put beside everything else.

Emotionally, the family was all over the map. Members we'd get to know were like characters out of classic literature, a mix of Anna Karenina and Kafka, with a chaser of melancholy sweetness, à la Tennessee Williams perhaps. Right when you thought they had taken it too far you'd be stunned by an act of tenderness.

The ultra-national father ran the place with an iron fist. His wife was perpetually smoothing things over out of his earshot, and their daughter or daughter-aged relative shook everything back up for no apparent reason beyond entertaining herself. Another man in the family management circle acted as the wild card, playing both sides of the street at different times of the day. He might have been a brother, an uncle, or even an old family friend who came with them when they escaped the tyranny of war-torn Europe, only to have to deal with what the father described as the "polite oppression" that is . . . Canada?

After an animated rant about how his adopted nation couldn't do right by him if they signed over the entire country for the price of a cold beer—and America? Exponentially worse. Too much freedom, liberty gone amok until it was now only self-gratification and bad TV. He wandered off mid-sentence, a rake in hand, leaving his wife to do the actual registering and retail side of the operation.

"Can you tell me how much these are?"

I set the bag of marshmallows in front of her. The sticker was clearly labeled $10, but even in Canadian dollars it had to be a mistake.[54]

She tried to wait me out but finally came around a little, nodding toward her husband, who was walking around looking f leaves to take it out on.

"Only Lafka uses the price gun." She paused. "Giv it and we don't say a word."

Another nod in Lafka's direction. We'd tossed a dollar Canadian coin) on another store counter for th sugar the night before. By my estimation Lafka had everything marked up 400 to 600 percent. But then his wife didn't charge me for the kids to camp and whispered where to get some firewood left by the previous campers. I felt I was in a war movie, smuggling supplies past the guard. I imagined her a tightrope walker and Lafka trying to take down the safety net for the past thirty years.

Still, the place had an odd charm. The sun didn't appear for more

54. I walked into the store and walked right back out after finding a package of pasta would have set us back $12.

than five minutes during our stay and there was no beach, none of the sand or the umbrellas and the *Brighton Beach Memoirs* vibe I'd painted in my mind. Just a rocky waterfront and a splintery dock leading to fishing boats. Bobbing like corks every ten yards were harbor seals with cloudy doe eyes. Made you want to take one home. We were informed that their bites were much worse than their barks.

"Seals very bad. Don't feed," Lafka scowled. "Bit a man's hand off last summer. Bad for business, but protected so I can't shoot them. They try to eat my customers' catch. Maybe a few get killed with a boat propeller, eh?"

His daughter walked up to the docks with a hose and a scraper and at least half her body covered in tattoos.

"I feed them," she said in a stage whisper.

And that seemed to sum up her relationship with Lafka.

She was also the one who handed us our clubs and balls for putt-putt.

"Have fun, if you can."

This seemed an odd sendoff until we tried to play the first hole. Not only was the course built into a hill—most greens were level enough to play if a person hadn't been drinking and wasn't suffering an inner-ear infection—but the course gave new meaning to the expression *pulling the ball to the left or right*. Climbing was required to reach many holes, and if you overplayed the greens you didn't take a mulligan, you took a hike to find your ball somewhere down in the campground. Adding to the course difficulty was that it had not been groomed since 1978. The turf was home to rough patches, deep, angry divots. It also featured an uneven blanket of pine needles, leaves, and bark chips.

"You want to get our money back?" Beth asked. She'd volunteered to haul baby Matteo, riding him low on her back in the Ergobaby carrier, but it was still a push to carry a one-year-old uphill while trying to make par. Maybe she wanted an out.[55]

Quinn was beyond the age of reason, but in the angry center of the age of frustration. If there exists a game more maddening than golf, I challenge you to find it. My oldest son was not appreciating the dry-rot borders, bark chips, or leaves.

"We're pedaling three kids across Canada. A few pine needles and bit of a slope isn't gonna stop us," I said.

Quinn glared.

"Ah, Dad. How do we count this?"

Quinn's ball was over the hole, but there was too much debris to let it drop in.

That's when we saw Lafka's wife coming to the rescue. Rather, we heard her before we saw her, powering up a gas-fed leaf blower.

She topped the rise in goggles, a traditional Polish outfit of puffed long sleeves and Technicolor skirt, and something that could have been a jet-pack strapped to her back. Seeing her storming in our direction made me think of a collision between Joseph's coat of many colors and an extra from those *Road Warrior* movies.[56]

---

55. Maybe I didn't want Joe to feel bad when I beat him by ten strokes. Matteo was giving me an edge, helping with my balance and correcting my swing by leaning out to see the colorful balls roll around.

56. If anything, Joe is downplaying her appearance. If the symphony battle music from Apocalypse Now, when the helicopters come in over the water, had been playing as she came up that hill, it couldn't have been dramatic enough.

Sporting a determined smile, she waved us off to the side of the course. When Lafka's wife cranked that leaf blower to full, I feared it would send the little yard-gnome-sized woman off the mountain,[57] but she held firm, like a firefighter to the flame, clearing out the courses and greens of unwanted chips, leaves, and needles. If nations applied that woman's no-nonsense work ethic and her diplomatic skills we could eliminate the United Nations and the IMF. She'd completed eighteen holes before we'd played through the fourth. Only then could we speak to one another again.

"Fore," I yelled in an exaggerated, theatrical voice before tapping the ball as gently as I could toward the base of the windmill. At least, I think it was a windmill, its paint having chipped away from its facade years ago. Two of its three blades remained.

"I'll go after your ball if it jumps the rails, Mom," Enzo offered.

On the back nine Beth said, "I think this is the most fun we've ever had playing putt-putt."

We'd take on half a dozen more putt-putt courses before the end of the road trip, but none of them came close.

Beth made friends with a mother who, with her own rugrats, had buckets of fish heads to offer as playthings. My kids added plastic lightsabers to the mix and hours of fish-gut-covered-projectile fun ensued. I knew we'd pay dearly on the road—the smell of fish guts never comes fully clean from wool sweaters or any clothing, as it happened—but that

---

57. I feared it would send one of my boys over the mountain.

ship had sailed already, so I let go.[58]

Lafka leaned hard on his rake, scowling when the pack of kids ran by with fish heads speared atop lightsabers on their way to feed the seals.

On our way out, Lafka discovered that my last name was Polish. (It's Lithuanian, but I wasn't going to correct the man, what with him coming around the counter for a big bear hug. Besides, half his customers thought he was Russian, so it was one big confused Benetton commercial by then anyway.)

"You come back every summer!" He looked around for something to give me, something with no market value. I could see his eyes darting around the store.

He settled on a collection of Sunny Beaches postcards showcasing it during its heyday. The putt-putt course sparkled, the docks gleamed, and there a much younger Lafka posed behind the wheel of a boat, trying his best not to scowl at the camera: PRODUCTION COPYRIGHT 1981.

I carried those postcards all the way to the end of our adventure, and will carry those crazy Russkies in my heart and funny bone forever.

---

58. Quinn's sweater was the worst. We washed it in bleach and expensive detergents. I hated to do it but I finally threw it away and told everyone it had gotten lost.

Chapter 8

Ruckle Park: Fellowship of the Fire Ring

The Road goes ever on and on
Down from the door where it began,
Now far ahead the Road has gone,
And I must follow if I can

—J. R. R. Tolkien, *The Lord of the Rings*

After conquering the length of the Galloping Goose rail-trail, we crashed with Steve and Mel for another few nights in Victoria. Beth wanted to tour Butchart Gardens, but also, it marked our last chance to leave anything we didn't need, get tips and pointers for our ride up the island, and let Beth experience one of the best parts of bike touring: the sharing of stories, retelling the ride, working the adventures out into the light and having others reflect your experiences and add to the tales with some of their own.

If you're with touring cyclists, it can blow the evening wide open—drinks come out from the good part of the pantry, tales trigger other stories with lots of hand gestures, and at one point someone will run out to the garage to bring in a bike-related prop, visual aid, or punch line.

Steve and Mel couldn't believe how fast Beth was taking to it.[59]

"But Canada's a big country, Joe," Steve said. It was the next morning. We were standing in his shed, working pedals onto one of my son's crank arms. "She's had a good start, but keep babying her until Beth comes into her own. Light panniers and encouraging words."

Steve would go on to give us crackpot advice concerning cougars and the topography of Salt Spring Island, but the man knew women and, more importantly, women riding partners. His words regarding Beth: gospel.

We wanted to make the afternoon ferry to Salt Spring Island. It was an easy thirty miles on more rail-trail, fresh fruit stands, and a few back roads to the docks north of Sydney.[60]

"When we make landfall, should we look for a camp spot in that first town, or can we make this Ruckle Park you keep raving about?"

No one disputes what Steve said next. "There's one big climb out of the harbor, then it's flat and fast the rest of the way to Ruckle. You'll make it before tea."

59. I was putting on a good front. But there had been a fire lit somewhere in there.
60. I remember how casual we were about the pace and how many times we stopped. All based on the fact that once we hit the ferry it would be a piece of cake to the island campground.

❧

So much for Steve babying Beth. But the debacle leading up to the ferry—involving five lanes of traffic, four different unmarked boats, and a husband dead-set on making the 2 PM departure—that was on me.

I should have waited, but I figured if one of us made it to the dock and bought the tickets, they might hold the departure. I carefully worked my way across five lanes of slowing traffic, using hand signals and coming into the terminal, easy as pie.[61] I expected Beth to follow my lead. She was having none of it. I watched my rearview in helpless frustration as she followed the side road,[62] which would eventually bring her to the docks but, in my estimation, not in time to make the ferry.

Then my plan really fell apart. We couldn't get down to the boats except by elevator, and we couldn't go back the way we came. With the speed of an Indy pit crew, I disconnected our contraption at the Trail-A-Bike. Somehow, using luck, smoke, and mirrors, I managed to force it and the boys into an elevator. David Copperfield would have been proud. The lift spat us out onto a busy tarmac. We reassembled our mule train, suited back up, and rolled between lines of idling cars to where a stream of pedestrians waited to board a ferry. Exhausted, but happy to be in line, I thought of Beth for the first time in a while.

The clock was counting down. I'd buy our tickets on board, but we had to wait for Beth. I stood on the trailer to see over the crowds and cars. I was spooked, then relieved and miffed when she rolled up

61. That's a load o' crap. I saw him power across the highway like he owned the roads.
62. If by *side road* Joe is referring to the bike path with the sign reading BIKES: THIS WAY TO FERRIES.

behind me.[63]

I launched into a speech about taking the lane, being an assertive rider, and the inflexibility of ferry schedules.

"There's a few things you need to know," Beth said. "Like you're about to get on the wrong boat and I've already bought the tickets for the right one. At least I think it's the right one. I was too busy looking for you to be sure. Oh, and just for the record, I got a petty thrill watching you wrestle everything out of the elevator, but I feel a little bad about that now, if it means anything."

It did. I so wanted to be her man most of the time that I went off half-cocked, but usually with the best intentions.[64]

She smiled, letting me know it wasn't all my fault.[65]

"Look, I know it runs in my family, cutting it too close at airports and all," Beth said. "And that works you into an even more spastic bull-in-a-china shop frenzy than you would be in already."

The boys nodded. They'd seen this time management tug-of-war between their parents often. Sometimes I'd get them to a station with hours to kill, sometimes Beth had them in a dead sprint.

Beth offered up a memo of understanding. "I'd rather catch the next boat, train, plane, or pack mule than split up again."

I started to relax, handing out water bottles to the boys. So it surprised me to see Beth clipping back in. "I didn't mean now! We still need to catch the right boat."

Another chaotic push across the terminal, but this time we never

63. Ferry tickets for a family of five: $46. Seeing your husband balancing on the back end of a bike trailer with a look of constipated frustration on his face: Priceless.
64. Road to hell, people, paved with them.
65. Sure it was, but he'd suffered enough.

lost sight of each other.

The hill out of the harbor looked nearly vertical, but we took our time shopping in the little store by the docks. Since we'd been assured it was the only climb we faced between there and Ruckle Park, we even stopped to pose for folks we'd met on the ferry.

Many people couldn't get over the audacity of our adventure. Then there were the ones who wanted documentation for when they told the story later.

A retired schoolteacher who'd toured by bike for much of his life was nearly overcome with emotion.

"You don't know how much I wanted to do this with my kids when they were young."

He bear-hugged us, then turned to the boys. "You are the future."

Enzo got onto the Trail-A-Bike. "No, we're the Kurmaskies."

With that, we headed for the hill.

I kept us upright, but it took all my focus and gearing skills. Heading into the steepest part of the grade, I heard Beth call from behind us for an all-stop.

"I think I broke my chain."

If I let up even a little we'd be walking the mule train the rest of the way, but after recent events I had to stop. I left the boys and the train in the grass and started trotting toward Beth.

"Oops," she said. "I think I was just in a really low gear so it felt broken."

She giggled as she pedaled past. I slogged back up to the bike and we walked to the top.[66] Beth was waiting. There were hills stretching into the distance.

"The future looks hard," I said.

"And I thought Steve was a good guy. Why would he lie like that to fellow cyclists?" Beth said.[67]

"Maybe he was thinking of a different island," Enzo offered.

This is why I don't like people telling me what to expect next. I'd have been fine except I set my mind for flat and fast.

"Can't you just reboot your brain, Dad?"

Quinn said this matter-of-factly. Like it was something he did all the time. So that's what I did. I saw the world for an instant with the big blue mind of a child and shot through the gap.

The hills didn't shrink, it's just that our good cheer grew. It didn't hurt to toil on a road lined with the soft fresh aromas of a summer afternoon, big trees, inviting lakes, and wildflowers catching the angle of the sun just so.

Somewhere along the line we decided to forgive Steve. But for every hill we walked the last ten yards of, I told the boys that our lying Canuck would owe us a slice of pizza.

Beth didn't even ride her brakes too hard on the steep descent into Ruckle Park. "This is too much fun," she called out. We had ourselves a need-for-speed convert.[68]

---

66. Not my proudest moment. But the chain really did feel broken, maybe because I'd never gotten it into that low of a gear. When I could spin the pedals that fast I just assumed I'd snapped the chain.

67. Later, Steve would tell us that he was just trying to give us encouragement and maybe we wouldn't notice the smaller bumps after the first big one.

68. I still rode the brakes pretty hard, but it was a moment in the ride I remember thinking I could do this . . . I was doing it. It felt like a test I'd just passed.

Every campground in the world would do well to switch over to the Ruckle Park floor plan and philosophy. Cars had at be left in a central lot. All camping was bike-or-hike-in only. You grabbed a wheelbarrow and rolled supplies through an enchanted stretch of forest until you stepped beyond the trees and into another land.

By making the campground car-free, everything changed. Not only did it affect what people brought, it shifted how they treated each other. The campground was on a point. Grassy fields offered a panoramic view of the Strait of Georgia. The rocky shores a few yards below the point were teeming with starfish and other tide-pool creatures. Communal fire rings meant you could join the party or eat cold food in the dark. Bathrooms and showers were tucked back in the forest a few hundred feet.

"You don't need to buy any firewood tonight," said the campground host, looking like a miniature version of Santa Claus. "So many people have bought wood today, you should just save your contribution for tomorrow night's fires."

"It's the fellowship of the fire ring," Quinn said.

I couldn't have put it better. People shared food, conversation, extra camp chairs. Someone brought out a guitar. A few families with a mess of kids from New Zealand produced plastic lightsabers. Seconds later our boys brandished theirs.

It felt like a homecoming. People wanted to hear about our adventures. I looked across the fields and loved seeing fifteen or more communal fires dotting the landscape, spaced far enough apart so that one yard party didn't interfere with the next.[69]

"How old is your little one?" someone asked.

Beth popped up from her plate as if she'd been shocked. I stopped mid-bite. We looked at each other.

69. This was one of my favorite places we found on our adventure, and that's saying something because Canadian campgrounds round out a number of my top ten favorite camping spots on the planet. Number one is still The Catwalk in the Gila Wilderness, New Mexico.

"This'll sound like we're the world's worst parents," Beth said, "but I think we both just remembered that it's Matteo's birthday."[70]

We weren't fishing for a free, warmed-over piece of pie and a clap along from the staff of TGI Friday's. We'd honestly let it get by us.[71]

As it happened, one of the ten kids from New Zealand was celebrating a birthday that week, or had held off celebrating until he could be reunited with his friends. The mother had wheeled in not one but two cakes complete with candles. There's a name for these kinds of people . . . good parents.

They relit the candles and Matteo got to experience the ritual, that of scaring the poop out of a one-year-old. Every birthday babe always goes wide-eyed and still in the presence of group clapping, off-key singing, and a flaming wheel of sugar held near their face.

It cooled off quickly ten yards beyond the fire ring. A group of us stayed up after the last kid had dropped off to sleep. We took turns stirring the glowing coals. No one wanted to put on another log, since the flames would compete with a rare early-August meteor shower taking place over our heads.

Beth put her head on my shoulder. I slipped a hand into her back pocket, happy after all that I'd hauled her cute jeans along.[72]

---

70. I didn't forget his birthday! Joe was supposed to have gotten him something we could light on fire and eat, but then the hills distracted us. But let the record show that I never forgot his birthday.

71. Joe here—Let the record show that I forgot.

72. It's easy to be in love in the summertime, in cute jeans with the right man, even if that man would have sailed off to points unknown with my children in tow, if it weren't for me. But then, I wouldn't have been on Salt Spring Island, or on the adventure of my life, without him.

Chapter 9

The Battery King of British Columbia

In everyone's life, at some time, our inner fire goes out. It is then burst into flame by an encounter with another human being. We should all be thankful for those people who rekindle the inner spirit.
—Albert Schweitzer

Salt Spring Island Steve, the Battery King of British Columbia, gave us that look.

He stood at the edge of his wraparound porch, a priceless view of a hidden harbor over his shoulder.

I loaded the last of the gear. It was sunrise, but with the rest of Canada ahead of us, it was never too early to load out. Steve reminded me of a bird dog discovering that the big hunt's been called off.[73]

Surrounded by an embarrassment of riches, my newfound friend was a study in longing: a fleet of sleek vintage Vespa scooters in the garage, designer porch furniture worth a year's tuition at one of your better prep schools, a pristine Montello Pierre that some cycling legend pedaled to a stage win over the Pyrénées—back when riders drank and smoked *and* changed their own tires during a race—but Steve was thinking, "Let me come along and I'll strike a match to all of it."

He'd been so kind to us, which made crushing his spirit that much worse. It was not my decision, though. Steve's desire was something palpable, and he certainly had the gear. Hell, at fifty-two years old, training three times a week, rain or shine, his quads were those of a man half his age. But it was the good life that had boxed Steve in from all sides.

The Battery King of British Columbia was loyal, tender, and true to those around him. The very qualities that would have made him the perfect riding partner held him in place.

"She'd draw up divorce papers before we had the ferry schedules fig-

---

73. Steve was pitiful up there. I wanted to smuggle him into one of our bags.

ured out," he noted, "but what I wouldn't give . . ." His wife was out of town so we had no way of assessing Steve's statement except through the prism of our own marriage. Steve struck me as a wise man who wanted to stay married.

He was down off the porch, helping balance our monstrous rig while I strapped a stray rain jacket to the back rack and distributed breakfast bars to my crew.

"Oh, man . . . this must weigh a couple of hundred pounds!"

I told the boys to get on so Steve could feel the full effect.

"Hallelujah! Why not push two full-sized Harleys across Canada without turning on the engines?" He shook his head while slapping my back a few times, camaraderie as much as to assure himself that I was actual flesh and bone.

"Like wrestling an angry badger," he said, testing it around the driveway. I knew this was part of the appeal for him. It's why we'd gotten on like brothers separated at birth.

"You want to help push us up the hill?" There wasn't enough distance before the incline to pedal away unassisted, and Steve would do anything to put off the departure.

"Wanna tell Beth about the guy who joined your lunch ride last week?" I asked Steve.

"For years folks talked about Roger like the guy won the Tour de France in a parallel universe or something. It's a small island, but no one in any circle had seen him on a bicycle."

"Until last week," I piped in.

Steve smiled. We'd reached the top of the hill.

"We're always inviting Roger to ride with us, but of course he never does . . . until last week. He rumbles through the parking lot in a beater truck, but showroom-new compared with the Nishiki he hauls from its bed. We stand in stunned silence watching him prepare for our loop. I see cobwebs, actual webs with leaves and stuff stuck under the seat, and more webs between spokes.

"He's in cutoff shorts and a KISS ME I'M IRISH (he's not) T-shirt. He kicks the tires a few times before opening a can of motor oil. My entire crew flinches at this. Some of us make sounds you hear when a high-wire artist stumbles. Roger takes no notice. Maybe the football helmet he's wearing blocks out all sound.

"All I'm thinking is that one of my pals put him up to this. It's an elaborate joke that will end when he reaches into his truck and pulls out the real bike.

"The oil makes a *gunk, gunk* sound as it spills over the freewheel. Roger's hand motions are those of someone dressing a salad. He douses the chain ring and some of links with liberal amounts of Pennzoil before putting on oversized gardening gloves, mounting this relic, and asking if we're ready. If we're ready!

" 'I might wait at the state park entrance if anyone drops off my pace,' he says.

"While we laugh, Roger, in his Converses and rusty toe clips, lights out like a time-trial contender. We scramble to clip in and shove off, expecting that our football hero—rumor has it he played semi-pro ball down in the States at one time—will burn himself out by the second bend or the first hill.

"Never happens. We formed a tight paceline and worked as if sponsored, but the best we managed was to spot that bright orange helmet a few times between here and the ferry. After that, we lost him completely.

"I fostered a story about Roger ducking out early on so that his myth wouldn't grow any larger and mess with our heads . . . you can't have a long-standing lunchtime group ride destroyed by one man in gardening gloves, high-tops, and syrupy motor oil. On the upside, someone noticed that, as a unit, we'd crushed our best time by more than five minutes."

Beth wouldn't have related two weeks ago; now she was riveted.

"I guess everyone needs a Roger," I said.

Steve let go of my handlebars. "You guys are my Roger now."

"Hardly," I noted. We shared a group hug as the sun broke through the trees. My family assumed their positions.

"Can I get a football helmet?" Enzo asked.

I answered by silently pushing off. We needed no more than a pedal stroke to tuck and go for broke down the biggest hill on the island. Victory tuck: one hell of a start to any morning. Over our hoots and yahoos, I swore I heard Steve's cheers join the mix, but by the time I chanced a peek, he was gone.

Chapter 10

James and His Giant Peach Bicycle

Well, I believe in the soul, the small of a woman's back, the hanging curve ball, high fiber, good scotch, that the novels of Susan Sontag are self-indulgent, overrated crap. I believe Lee Harvey Oswald acted alone. I believe there ought to be a constitutional amendment outlawing Astroturf and the designated hitter. I believe in the sweet spot, soft-core pornography, opening your presents Christmas morning rather than Christmas Eve and I believe in long, slow, deep, soft, wet kisses that last three days.
—Crash Davis, *Bull Durham*

Nothing so large and exuberant had ever gotten the jump on me, at least not in broad daylight, during good weather while riding a bicycle with not one but three clean, unobstructed views through rear-facing mirrors.

Still, there he was, just off to my left as if beamed in from the planet of gigantic Irishmen. James the massive Celtic warrior atop a towering peach-colored mountain bike, front basket made of wicker and a silver bell he was overly fond of ringing after making a salient point or just because he was apeshit happy . . . which was most of the time about everything: sunlight, the sound of gravel under his wheels, the act of breathing.

We'd finally met someone more excitable than me.

"That's absolutely brilliant!" Everything James said came with an exclamation point. "Can't say I've ever happened onto anyone pedaling such a substantial getup over hills . . . and by the looks of it, for distance! Brilliant!"

"Holy crap!" For a seven-year-old, Enzo used exclamation points in acceptable doses, unless sugared up or describing a Legos creation he'd devoted hours to. Given that a shirtless giant with a full head of red hair, graying thicket of beard, matching bath mat of chest hair, Speedo in the colors of the Italian flag, and hiking boots was matching our cadence a few feet off the starboard bow, I seconded Enzo's emotions and let my son's language breach slide.

Quinn shook his head and smirked. Just another day at Road Scholar U.

By way of greeting, I bumped fists lightly with our flying Irishman at seventeen miles an hour. He liked that. We exchanged names, followed by the standard who, what, and whatnot. That's where the conversational path diverged in the wood. During a brief lull James broke into song: "The Night Pat Murphy Died." His voice matched his body. Massive and surprisingly tender but all over the page.

"Nice pipes," Quinn shouted up to me during the chorus.

"No self-control," I yelled back. Looking at the man again, I added, "Or pants."

Quinn cracked up.

If James heard me, he took no notice.

By the third verse, Enzo was singing along with the chorus. God knew my son could use some distractions and merriment. We'd been through four, maybe five microclimates before noon. The morning thunderstorm bashing waves along the seawall had left Enzo mud-slathered and salt-sprayed. Both mud and salt had dried, leaving raised blotches across the length of him. Occupational hazard. The Trail-A-Bike rider wears more of the road trip than everyone else aboard. Even with a stiff plastic pebble guard, much of the day's events would end up smeared and splattered over his clothes and up his back.

Seems that when the world treats you like a rolling Jackson Pollock canvas, singing helps.

By the time James caught our rear wheel, the sun was out in force, but it was by no means Speedo weather.

Quinn pointed this out. Or he called attention to the country colors James was covering his private bits with.

"You wear our flag, but you don't sound Italian."

James rang his bell with extra gusto, pedaling closer to Quinn, sizing him up proper. This would have frightened lesser men but not my continental drifters.

"I like your eye for detail, son. Name?"

"Quinn!"

"The Mighty Quinn," Enzo added.

"Well done," James noted, smiling over his shoulder at Enzo. "Always talk up your brother, always stand by his side." Two quick rings of the bell. No one could argue with that. We pedaled along, matching cadences for a few hundred yards, pondering brotherhood.

"Quinn. A good Irish name, but you're defending Italy's colors."

"Mom's Italian, Dad's Irish," Quinn said.

"Dad's a mutt actually," I said. "But a good chunk of it circles back to Ireland."

James let loose a surprised whistle, as if he'd made a real find: dinosaur bone or human head.

"You're ten/two splits, then! I wouldn't want to go against you boys on a soccer field or a bar stool."

James: big, bold, brassy, more than a little inappropriate, and sporting a gold tooth like a pirate. Just the sort you rarely meet outside a long bike ride. And because we were on wheels I felt confident we could move on down the road at a quick clip if he turned out to be rabid rather than delightfully excitable.

"I wear the Italian flag out of respect for our most formidable rival on the playing field . . . besides, my kilt was off to the cleaners!"

He winked at Enzo.

"But it's too cold for a Speedo," Enzo countered.

James shook his head vigorously. "This be Canada in August, lads. If not now, when?"

That gave us a good laugh. If I'd had a bell I might have rung it. James's mood was contagious, and we'd been on the road long enough to embrace it.

"Let's play some 'I believe,' " James said. It wasn't as much a request as a call to order. "It'll put us in an exuberant mood," he added.

As if more exuberance were possible, but I was willing to try. Only I had no idea what game he was talking about.

"We trade on things we believe, the only rule, try for profound one round, sublime the next."

I shoved a confused squint at the massive Irishman.

"Did you see the movie *Bull Durham*?"

I sighed at the mere thought. A thoroughly satisfying two for one: baseball and buddy flick. I especially loved the scene where Costner tossed out that list of things he believed in to impress Susan Sarandon . . .

"I know how to play now . . . ," I said.

James erupted like a howler monkey, cranked off a few rings of the bell before diving into the game. If he had a brake on that bike or on himself, James hadn't engaged it around us yet. He cleared his throat.

"I believe everyone should nap under a palm tree at least once, and pee out-of-doors often."

Enzo chuckled.

James nodded over to me.

"I believe . . . the combination of lyrics, keyboards, percussion, and guitars on the Who's 'Teenage Wasteland' saved me from breaking bad every single day of high school."

James smacked his handlebar. "Of course it did!"

He turned to Quinn. The pause was so long I thought that perhaps Quinn was unclear on the rules of the game.

"I believe . . . you should consider pants," Quinn said.

Our Kevlar caravan burst into sustained laughter.

James shook his fist in mock rage and rang his bell.

It was on now.

Enzo stopped pedaling the Trail-A-Bike to consider his contribution. Fortunately, the Trail-A-Bike isn't tied in to the tandem's drive train because the little man stops pedaling for any number of reasons: interesting roadkill, a particular cloud formation that's caught his eye . . . all activities I consider his inalienable rights as a child, especially one repeatedly recruited into his dad's unorthodox travel adventure projects.

"I believe . . . I'll always want another dance."

Boy's his own Soul Train program. Soundtrack or not. Find Enzo some cardboard, a beat, and the little man's golden.

James kicked off the next round.

"I believe . . . in facing into the season's first cold wind, searching for the moon every night . . . and spending whatever it takes on proper footwear."

Hell yes! I thought. We grunted our approval in unison. He *was* sporting a solid pair of hiking boots jammed into toe clips. A rather clunky footwear selection, but then he wasn't carrying a small third-world country behind his bike.

My turn.

"I believe jealous hearts and worried minds never held anything together."

James took a closer look, sizing me up. Like maybe there was a bit more cortex than spinal cord helming this operation after all.

"Now you tell me!"

"I believe . . ." Quinn waited for our full attention. "That William Shatner was the only captain who didn't need special effects to command a starship."

Silence. James nodded vigorously. Enzo laughed.

"That's what I'm talking about!" I yelled into the BC afternoon.

James and his game had me using exclamation points now. From Priceline to cheesy legal dramas on network television, The Shat was unstoppable. A real force of nature. I flashed on him wrestling a young Ricardo Montalban in *The Wrath of Khan* before Enzo pulled me back from my Trekkie daydream.

"I believe peaches should never be put into a can." We'd had roadside stand fresh fruit the day before. Enzo had worn the evidence of juicy peaches on his face well into the next day.

"Good rule for fruit in general," James said. "Unless you're canning for personal use over a winter. I can't tell you how much canned crap they made us eat in the service."

We pedaled along for a stretch. No doubt thinking about fresh fruit and James's military service.

"I believe . . ." James paused, which was something new from him. "I believe it's better sometimes not to know the odds or the reasons."

We locked eyes at seventeen miles an hour. For a few seconds I thought I could see behind his, to the darker corners. His shoulder sported a USMC tattoo. The scar running the length of his thigh was unmistakably made by a bullet. He offered the slightest nod. Before I could ask anything he winked, rang the bell, and announced, "Lightning round. Ten seconds on the clock."

The boys loved this guy. Bipolar perhaps, but he brought it: crackling energy, games on demand, and more than a pinch of danger on the fly. Get in a car on a Friday after work with James and you'd come back with some stories, or you might not come back at all.

He looked at me.

"And . . . go."

I breathed deep, like a contender about to start a breakaway.

"I believe in peak oil, short skirts, cantaloupe, Italian food cooked by Italians . . . and that only some of us get what we deserve."

Quinn came right back with, "I believe in wall ball, climbing too high in trees, most of the music my dad put on my iPod, and that Dots better not be the ice cream of the future."

"They're all air, no cream," Enzo whined. "What a gyp."

"Ten seconds," James prompted my middle son.

"I believe in wall ball, too, summer vacation, bike rides across countries, s'mores with the mellows browned but not burned, and Mom's good night kisses."

I don't know why the last bit cut me so deep.

Make no mistake, I've known since the night that Alliston Dwyer left me standing in the darkness of a country club golf course, thinking that I loved her with all my ninth grader's heart only to have her come back to steal a final kiss, that life will try to break you, and often succeed. But having boys who let you inside their heads, who hand over their hopes and their well-being, trusting you to safeguard them while they go about trying to be kids, trusting you enough to get themselves up each day of a bike tour, to keep pedaling just because their dad asks them to . . . well, love that bone-marrow-deep is the only force I know capable of breaking your fall.

"Your turn, Mr. James," said Enzo. We'd almost reached the top of a long, steady climb. The type that, if you're talking, goes unnoticed until you look behind you. The water was on our right, thick evergreen forest on our left, as James slowed the pace for the first time since we'd met.

"I believe . . . lads like you three give me some good reasons to carry on."

James rode a bike for reasons that had nothing to do with garden-variety exercise, on this one thing I was sure.

"Four," Quinn pointed out. "Our baby brother's back there sleeping in the trailer."

James peered into the chariot as we slowed at the crest. An incredulous look appeared on his face.

"Brilliant." His voice down just above a whisper for the first time.

"Bonus round," he shouted, then launched right in.

"I believe . . . you could best me to the top of the next rise if you had the mind to. Object lesson on balls and vigor. That's what you boys turned out to be."

Enzo took the bait. "You're on."

I shifted to our second hardest gear; Quinn timed his pedal stroke as though he'd been stoking all his life. We got the jump on James, but he came roaring back. It's quite difficult to outpace a sixteen-foot, 438-pound bike train going downhill. James rang his bells as he went by on the rise. We'd used our momentum, every bit of team pedaling, and fluid downshifting to hold him off, but three-quarters of the way up he chugged by. His size cannot be overstated. When James spread his arms at the crest he resembled a condor about to catch a thermal updraft.

We finished out the climb as if it were a points sprint in the Tour de France. I thanked the boys for their effort, but that was lost in the parting waves to James. He looked back as he hit the flats, gave one more nod, then leaned over the straight bars of his mountain bike in a ridiculous effort to gain some aerodynamics.

But can't every effort be seen as ridiculous by someone?

"I believe that man's gonna make it," Enzo said.

Now, I know my son was referring to the distance to his car or home or wherever James was off to that day. And maybe he meant before weather or nightfall caught him. But it made me smile, thinking perhaps my boys and our own ridiculous effort reached something forgotten and unsullied within James and his giant peach bike . . .

Beth rolled up quiet as a ninja. Twice in one day I'd been caught from behind without an inkling. We took mercy on her, waiting at the top while she and two sweet and salty granola bars communed.

"Did you see that biker about as big as Paul Bunyan go by?" she got around to asking. "Gold tooth, no pants. Ringing his freakin' bell like a madman."

A silent signal passed between me and the boys, in this case a wink. I can always count on them for the harmless con.

"Wouldn't have missed something like that," Quinn said.

"Ring, ring."

Baby Matteo, with less than a ten-word vocabulary, sold us out.

"He was great," Enzo confessed. "We played 'I Believe' and sang 'The Night Pat Murphy Died.' It had some swear words in it."

I smiled at Beth.

"He was big as all outdoors, unstable, but not crazy."

She pedaled out, looking over her shoulder as she went.

"And you should know."

Chapter 11

Freefalling

I used to smoke marijuana. But I'll tell you something: I would only smoke it in the late evening. Oh, occasionally the early evening, but usually the late evening—or the mid-evening. Just the early evening, mid-evening and late evening. Occasionally, early afternoon, early mid-afternoon, or perhaps the late-mid-afternoon. Oh, sometimes the early-mid-late-early morning . . . But never at dusk.

—Steve Martin, "Marijuana"

You know you're in for it when a pair of guys who look like teamsters introduce themselves as Moose and The Dawg. We were enjoying a few hours at a ropes course and bungee-jumping mecca called Wild Play. Enzo was too young to complete the ropes course, but he seemed happy to eat some potato wedges while he watched others throw themselves off a suspension bridge, tempting death at the end of a big rubber band.

Quinn spent the better part of an hour climbing through the elaborate ropes and barrels and zip lines.

"That's a hell of a thing you guys are doing," Moose said.

He was walking around our rig. The Dawg was by his side. They reminded me, well, of no one. These two were true originals. Moose sometimes finished The Dawg's sentences, they joked like sixth graders, and when I asked their wives if this was them on vacation or how they acted all the time, they said, "No, this is them all the time."

They had their kids doing the courses and their wives supplying them with copious amounts of food from the snack bar. As we stood and talked about our route and how we should stop in and see them when we came through Quebec, The Dawg passed me over something. Was he smoking a joint in the middle of the day in view of fifty people? I declined. Pot and pulling a mule train are pretty much mutually exclusive activities, and I had another thirty miles to go before we'd call it a day.

"Don't you worry bout getting busted?" I asked.

They had a good laugh.

"This is Canada, eh? We don't beat people to death for being gay or black or both, either."

They spent the next few minutes telling me, without malice, all the things they didn't do in Canada.

"Don't get us wrong, we love your country. We just can't stand a lot of the people. Mostly the ones in charge," The Dawg said.

Moose took another hit. "And that's when we're stoned. We can't even visit your country sober," he added.

"But you're all right," The Dawg added. "Maybe things are coming round down there, eh?"

Maybe.

Chapter 12

Cross-Training

Run like hell and get the agony over with.

—Clarence DeMar

I entered a triathlon when I was seventeen. It did not end well. Conditioned, coordinated, and firing on all cylinders, I made a mockery of our family name. To be even a mild success in the trifecta of sporting endeavors, one must like to run, or at least tolerate it. Since I only light out when the police are chasing me, or I'm chasing after balls of various sizes and colors, I had no business at the starting line.

What lured me in was my love for two of the three categories. As much conviction as the singer, Meat Loaf had on the song "Two Out of Three Ain't Bad," he'd never entered a triathlon.

I'd held the title of Florida's fastest breast stroker two summers in a row. I was a lifeguard not just to impress girls, but because I was made for the water. I spent so much time in chlorinated pools that my blond, perfectly feathered hair had a green tint to it.

We know how I feel about the bike. I rode everywhere in ninety-five-degree temps and 100 percent humidity, often covered in box elder bugs that were attracted to Florida's blacktop, so by the time I'd completed the swim and pedal portions on race day it didn't seem like a fair fight. I was in the top ten coming off the bike. But the run wiped that grin off my face. By the time I had the finish line in sight, old ladies were walking by, chitchatting, exchanging recipes and whatnot.

I probably should have run a few times during training. But I always felt so good after cross-training from the water to the wheel. Why wreck it with a humiliating run?

Triathlon memories hit me riding north on Vancouver Island: the elation of jumping so far out in front only to be pulled back by an activity that should have been eliminated eons ago by natural selection.

You either outran the saber-toothed tiger in the first fifty yards, found a hole in the rocks, climbed a tree, or were out of the gene pool. No caveman ever asked another what his PR time was, or how his shin splints were doing.

I can make a show of the sprint, but a hundred yards is my outer limit. After which, I take on the face of a constipated Willie Loman squinting into the distance for the sale that will never come. My arms pump with no discernible rhythm while I wheeze along like an asthmatic badger, oxygen-deprived and mad as hell about it.[74]

Canada's system of water park facilities started it all. Five alone on Vancouver Island. As a nation, they are well aware that summer is a passing fling, so the Canucks build towering indoor swim palaces. Not simple lap pools with roofs, maybe a wading pool thrown in as an afterthought, but aquatic cathedrals where true believers are baptized year-round in wave pools, spouting fountains shaped like pirate ships and killer whales, five-story slides—color-coded for pitch and speed— some of which even shoot outside then back in again on a serpentine loop of water fun. There are rope swings, diving platforms, current pools, and cascading waterfalls.[75]

The size of an average Costco, these meccas to Neptune rose up along the horizon. Ubiquitous as grain elevators in Iowa. The first time we stopped for a swim I was prepared to drop twenty bucks a person, which would have been the floor back home.

"It's ten dollars."

I handed over two twenties.

"Do you count the baby?"

She handed me back thirty.

"It's ten . . . for the family."

I gazed out at acres of water fun through the window behind her. Canada continued to strike me as not so much another country, but an

74. It's not pretty.
75. These were lifesavers. Just when the riding would get too much we'd find another water park. Quinn could spot one from five miles away.

entirely different dimension. In my lifetime it had provided the trinity—Aykroyd, Candy, Belushi—and now this.[76, 77, 78, 79]

We'd put in thirty-five miles on the bikes. A chance to cool down and soak some sore muscles had a decadent ring to it. I spotted a hot tub the size of Delaware off to the left.

Those same sore muscles, and heaps of others, were called into service during a three-hour water aerobics session known as parenthood. We staged lap races, swung from ropes, surfed the wave pool, and perfected flips from the low diving board.

But the activity that brought on the burn and brought back the memories of cross-training involved the older boys clinging to my back and shoulders in an effort to sink me, while I pushed a life-jacketed one-year-old atop a paddle board through the current course. In waist-high water, I assumed a squatting position to gain any leverage, then jogged through the rushing resistance while the boys took their best shots.

Professional football squads should consider it for spring training.

Each time I threw in the towel, they begged for just one more lap. An hour vaporized before the five-story slide called them away like the sirens in Greek mythology. I was spent and too damn hot by then for the hot tub.[80]

Back on the bike I realized an absurd level of exhaustion. Nerve endings tingled and fired, a pulsing sensation came in waves; a lighter-

---

76. And I'd like to add one more name to that list: Jon Stewart.
77. Honey, I'm pretty sure he's from New York.
78. Nope, he's too smart and funny. I'm sure he's from Quebec.
79. No, baby, you're thinking of Michael J. Fox. Funny, also short, but less Jewish.
80. What Joe has conveniently left out is that I played with the boys the other half of the time. We were both hammered shit after a "swim" break.

than-air, out-of-body experience that failed at the last instant, followed by an Egyptian-slaves-laboring-on-the-pyramids-sized burden.

Muscles I didn't recall having reported for duty only to commence complaining immediately. The sort of fatigue that makes one laugh out loud so as to keep going. I consoled myself with one thought: *It beats running.* Then I realized I'd been running all afternoon, only in water.

The time had come. I'd been saving it the way Popeye holds back spinach. A secret weapon I'd read about in a fitness column. You know it's desperate measures when I seek solutions from a fellow writer; liars and miscreants, all of them, but this particular suggestion had come by way of a number of sources, over time, circulating like a chain letter. A friend of a friend of a rider swore by it, the sister of an Olympic decathlete said he stocked it by the case, that sort of thing. And then I read it waiting in a checkout line. You can't go wrong with that sort of research. But it sounded so strange it just might work.

Chocolate milk.[81]

I limped our bike train into a gas station, sent Beth in with specific instructions to load up on chocolate milk while I panted over the handlebars and tried to think happy thoughts.

"What brand?" she asked.

"Doesn't matter," I mumbled. We had twenty miles of rolling hills to the campground. This had better work.

The boys came out slurping Fudgsicles. Beth was nowhere to be seen.

"Your mom authorized that purchase?"

81. I tuned him out a little when he started talking about the healing powers of chocolate milk, again. Who drinks milk on a bike ride?

The boys nodded. Animal fear gripping them.

I shook mine.

When Beth strolled out five minutes later carrying a Creamsicle I ambushed her.

"What in God's name is all this?"

I was getting worked up.

"I said chocolate milk. Not Fudgsicles." The boys looked appalled. Like I might snatch their treats out of their hands. "Chocolate milk is supposed to be better than Gatorade, Shot Bloks, or Endurox R4 in balancing your system and aiding in recovery time between, during, and after exercise."

For no good reason, I assumed Beth had read the same fitness column. It had sat, unmolested for months in the bathroom reading pile.[82]

She slammed down the pannier she'd been carrying, hoisted out a cute little jug of chocolate milk, and fumed while I looked it over.

I couldn't help myself. Blame it on fatigue or taking one's relationship for granted during times of stress.

"What took you so long in there, anyway?" Asked as casually as one inquires about the weather.

She pulled out a box of tampons, slammed them down on the big ice machine I'd been using to table the chocolate milk, and met my eyes.

"And you know what you can do with your magic chocolate milk, don't you?"[83]

---

82. I bring my own reading material into the bathroom. When you live with four boys it's the only way to be sure nobody's peed on it.
83. No, actually I wanted to pour it over his head, but what you were thinking would have been fine by me as well.

In this situation you want to follow government-issued duck-and-cover guidelines. Instead I took a long pull on the jug and blundered forward.

"Just wanted everyone to recharge on chocolate milk, not sugar up then crash a mile down the road . . . Jesus."

What Jesus had to do with electrolyte balancing I had no idea. Sometimes he's a teacher, more often in our family he's a misplaced punctuation mark.

Beth's rebuttal had the slow-building power of a storm surge. It began with how we weren't in the army, I was under some serious delusions of being in charge, this ride had been sold as a good time, and yes, children do enjoy chocolate milk, unless they are required to drink large amounts on a schedule.

It ended with, "You're a jackass. I'm going back to the bathroom so set your watch to suffering, 'cause it's gonna take as long as it takes."[84]

The boys looked away, clearly enjoying their Fudgsicles now that there was no danger of losing them.

At least the chocolate milk seemed to be kicking in. I felt ready to pedal to the eastern seaboard at that moment. Though it was more likely the shame and indignation coalescing inside me.

When she returned, Beth swigged from the jug and shot me daggers.[85]

Bill Murray once admonished a groundhog not to drive angry. The same can't be said for closing out the hard, late miles of a day on a

84. The only parts I remember saying were jackass and set your watch to suffering, but the rest of it sounds about right.
85. With the hot fury of a thousand suns.

bicycle. Anger is good. Anger could be the next sports drink. Anger will put you over the line. There's your tag line, Madison Avenue.[86]

But anger wasn't what put me so far ahead of Beth at our destination. Fatigue and signs for Hanging Garden Campground kept calling me forward. I was going too fast, with my head down just wanting to get us done. In my defense, I feared my muscles would seize up for good if I stopped again.

Beth was not in sight and I couldn't say when I'd seen her last. We waited at the top of the hill a hundred yards inside the entrance . . . and waited some more, but Beth did not come into view.

"Dad," Enzo asked. "Does a chocolate fountain need to be plugged in?"

Having a front-row seat to a seven-year-old's thought process is like driving bumper cars on acid.[87]

Quinn offered an answer that bodes well for a public school education or his skills despite one. "You'd need some power source to move the chocolate around."

"What about heating it? The chocolate has to stay melted, doesn't it?" I added. They always suck me in.

"You could use solar panels," Quinn said.

Our round-table discussion on making a chocolate fountain mobile would have to wait. Beth had come into view and it wasn't a pretty sight. Hangdogging it over the handlebars, she'd overshot the entrance.

---

86. I'd buy that T-shirt.

87. It's one of my favorite parts of parenthood. The outstandingly ridiculous subjects covered in conversation with your children. What's even better is when it starts to become normal to ponder things like "Would Darth Vader still be menacing if he were the size of Yoda? Could they make elevators that go left and right? Wouldn't it make sense in karate to have the next color after black be a tie-dye of all the colors?

Fortunately, we knew this drill. We'd taken the same dead end to a turnaround cul-de-sac. It wasn't a long detour. I waited a few beats, but she didn't swing back.

The boys had already unloaded themselves and a few snacks. Helmets scattered on the ground with gloves next to them. I decided to leave them be. I'd put my people through enough.

"I'm going after her. It's a cul-de-sac, so she won't be far. Quinn, you have the conn. Whatever you do, don't let your baby brother out of the trailer until I get back."

"On foot?" Quinn asked.

Seeing his father break into a run was like observing elephants painting at the zoo, businessmen wearing shorts at a company retreat, or Mennonites swearing from the front seat of a sports car.

As I ran, I allowed guilt to well up. She'd never believe this had nothing to do with our chocolate milk tiff. My pain distracted me, but she wouldn't buy it; I'd left her in the dust too often. I wanted to explain my failings when it came to cross-training. Like:

"It's like this, baby, I was never cut out to be a triathlete."

Looking none too steady in the saddle, she executed a shoddy dismount. I think I saw her wipe her eyes. Could have been sweat . . . The bike stayed where she'd dumped it, the back wheel spinning aimlessly.

Her shoulders shook. Yep, tears.[88]

Something remarkable happened at that moment, maybe for the first moment in my life. I ran hard, I ran fast, and for once I ran like

---

88. Sometimes you just need a good cry. Joe always wants to solve the problem when all it takes is good cry and his shoulder to lean against.

I'd been born to it. My arms found a rhythm, each step played off the other, momentum and bounce and a locomotive fury that saw me leave the earth a little with each stride. Be the gazelle . . .

Suck on that, triathletes, you smug, gaunt, hard-to-catch specimens of physical conditioning.

I eased up so as not to tackle the love of my life into the bushes. We held each other as if days and continents had come between us.

"I couldn't find you guys," she managed.

"It's a tricky turnoff."

She sniffled. "You left me. You keep leaving me."

I shook my head as if to say, *But I'm right here now*. Sometimes I've felt a longing for Beth in my life, even when she was standing right in front of me. I hadn't felt it on our bike trip until that afternoon.

I told myself that most of her tears were hormones, blood loss, the long day's ride, and low blood sugar talking, but after the rough patch our relationship went through shortly after the millennium, it felt like we could be talking in code here. We'd been closing the distances between us ever since. I didn't want a bike trip to muck it up.

"I won't do it again, I promise."

But the truth was when the suffering sets in like gangrene, it's hard not to get lost in the cadence. Whoosh, just like that, five kilometers get wiped from the memory banks like an alien abduction. Still, I would double my efforts when it came to keeping her in the rearview mirror.

"I really want to do this ride together . . . We're doing this thing together, understand?"

The heart has its own misunderstandings. Sometimes self-inflicted wounds confused for slights and the appearance of neglect. Sometimes real neglect. No matter the source, the heart can get lost, only to be found hours later wandering down dead ends with unexplained bruises and tears to its skin. I didn't want that for anyone I loved.

She'd come a long way as a cycling warrior in such a short time, and in our relationship. There was no justifiable reason to forget her halfway into battle. We'd been together most of our adult lives. I could say without hesitation that there weren't any finish lines I wanted to cross without her.

"I'm not talking about the bike ride," she said.

I squeezed her closer. "Good, 'cause I can't promise I won't zone out again."

Calmed, Beth pulled away from my shoulder.

"Hey, did you run for me . . . Jesus, you ran!"[89]

As if hearing it out loud made it real, my legs went rubber and my chest sucked in the full weight of the day.

"All the way, baby," I managed.

Beth knew how deeply I opposed running. How I like to tell people my Achilles' heel ran the length of my body. She recognized my badly choreographed *Chariots of Fire* imitation had taken all I had.

"So I can still make you breathless?"

Hands on my knees, I offered a pained smile. We were joking again. It almost made the run worth it.

"Where are the boys?"

I pointed back toward the entrance.

Beth went for her bike with firefighter's speed.

---

89. I still can't believe it. He must have used a stunt double.

"You can't just leave 'em by the side of the road," she said.

"There was a manned ranger's booth. And it's more of a path, really." I wanted to jog alongside her, but it was all I could do to walk upright. "I left 'em half a jug of chocolate milk and a map of Canada."

Beth flashed me her fake evil eye, the one that looks more like the sassy-haired girl in a Prell commercial.

"Not that I should tell you, but your asinine chocolate milk theory works. I'd be in a ditch otherwise."[90]

"It's not a theory . . . ," I shouted. But she was already pedaling up the hill, heading for the entrance.

Maybe it's all I ever needed to become a complete triathlete. I took another swig of the milk she'd left with me, imagining myself Popeye, then willed my legs to take off running, right by Beth and her loaded bike.

But there was nothing left down there, nothing but a lazy stride carrying me alongside Canadian pines near sunset.

Some dreams die hard.

Not this one, though. I've never been more comfortable inside my own skin, moseying along a rural road, pondering the virtues of chocolate milk, the comforts of a deserved sleeping bag, the consolation of being accomplished at two out of three athletic endeavors . . . and the sweetest of victories: the spoils of a real marriage pulled carefully, slowly and daily, back from the brink.

---

90. Who knew. You'd think it would make you want to throw up in the heat and exertion, but the chocolate milk won me over. Weeks later I have this fond memory of all four of us, still on our bikes, passing around one big jug of chocolate milk before riding on down the road. People, now that's living.

Chapter 13

Haircut of the Gods

That's business up front and party in the back to you.
—Anonymous

In a campground near Nanimo, Beth threw her hands up.

"We have to get these boys haircuts."

I tilted my head to one side for a better look at their locks as they chased some new friends across a jungle gym.

"I think I just saw something fly out of Enzo's rat's nest, and Quinn

MUD, SWEAT, AND GEARS

looks like Rod Stewart," Beth said.[91]

I hadn't given my son's heads a second thought, except for a vague recognition that it took longer to towel Enzo off these days after swimming, and Quinn was showing symptoms of a nervous disorder, always snapping his head to keep the bangs out of his eyes.

"Have you asked them how they feel about it?"

Beth looked at me like I was crazy.

"I know how they feel about it. They'd run around unbathed in dreadlocks, carving their toothbrushes into spears if I let them."

Most of the population of Burning Man flashed into my mind at that moment.[92]

"Fine by me. Just keep an eye out for a barbershop."

"Their hair's at the perfect length for killer mullets," Mr. M. said, hoping I'd make his day and ruin my boys' summer. Mullets were almost worth the look on Beth's face, but it would render all photos of the trip from here on state's evidence in the emancipation hearings.

We'd found our way into Curls and Cuts, a full-service styling center offering waxing, massages, tanning, and nail brushing—whatever that was—on the side.

I wanted to rename it "Trapped in Time Salon." This place was problematic for anyone in town who did not look upon the mid-1980s

91. I wasn't up on child neglect laws in Canada, but I was pretty sure someone in a government vehicle was going to pull up any moment, take a look at their hair, and haul my boys away from me forever.
92. For the record, Joe's never been to Burning Man, but we live in Portland, Oregon, so there's very little difference—unless you have a house in the West Hills, then you have my pity or envy, depending on the day.

as the golden age of hairstyles. When big hair roamed the earth and Jheri curls, wall and wave bangs, asymmetrical 'Nilla Ice cuts, and mullets dominated the pages of high school yearbooks.

Shelly, the owner, was an easygoing PTA mom with a headbanger's heart. You could imagine her slipping out of a school board meeting early to crank up Bon Jovi in the parking lot and burn one down, or just to remember when she would have. Her hair, which looked like someone had tossed a doormat onto her head and stapled it to her ears, couldn't have been good for business.

Mr. M. wore jeans found in the boys section of JCPenney, tucked into engineer's boots . . . and for a shirt, he'd decided on the flaming Phoenix airbrush pattern popularized across the hoods of black Trans Ams.

Surprisingly, no mullet. Instead, his long, lush brown hair was a dead ringer for Lady, the cocker spaniel in the Disney classic *Lady and the Tramp*.

Delores spoke in a gravelly baritone reserved for chain-smoking barmaids and truck stop waitresses.

By the looks of it, she'd been experimenting with the tanning equipment after hours to shocking results. In a bold move, she'd decided not to soften the effects of prolonged UV exposure with auburn or black hair, but used it as a springboard to showcase some of the biggest hair on the island. Dyed canary yellow and teased into unnatural shapes, it had no gravitational boundaries. Members of the band Spinal Tap would have taken one look and fallen to their knees.

I only caught a few glimpses of the woman who did the nails, but her hair was quite stylish, of this decade even. Which led me to believe she had it done out of house.

Beth was shopping with Matteo across the street. The next time she saw her boys she wanted very little hair on their heads. I gave Mr. M. the bad news. He took it well. While dressed like a muscle car decal, he turned out to be the consummate professional.

"I think we should go with The Caesar then. It's what the kids are wearing these days. A buzz cut, but I leave a tuft of hair a little longer in the front."

I gave it the green light. Shelly turned up Guns N' Roses and went to work on Enzo. When I looked up from an ancient magazine, Quinn was sporting a mullet so perfect I mistook it for a wig. It was freak-show glorious.

"Hey . . . ," I began, but I couldn't get beyond that.

The reason I referred to him as Mr. M. in my mind was that when Shelly introduced us, she'd fast-talked the name. All I heard was Mary. Nothing wrong with a hairdresser in a cocker spaniel do named Mary, but I didn't want to offend a man holding a pair of sharp scissors.

Shelly looked over, backing off of a laugh. "Cut it out, Murray," she said.

Murray, of course!

"You know these guys probably have another hundred kilometers to pedal before nightfall," she added.

We were five miles from camp.

"Yeah, Murray." Relaxed, joking with him. Relieved to finally know his name.

Murray looked sheepish, but proud. "I just wanted to see if I was right."

He spun Quinn around. "It's some of my best work . . . but I'll have it off in a few minutes."

A couple of strokes of the clippers and it was a memory, but I'd caught a glimpse of what I'd look like in a parallel universe. It surprised me how comfortable I appeared, sitting on my plaid couch, feet up on the cable spool coffee table, rewatching my boxed set of Chuck Norris in *Walker: Texas Ranger*.[93]

My hair had always been the right texture for a truly epic mullet. I'd be hurting no one if I let them show me that business in the front, party in the back guy before they shaved it off.

"I think I could use a trim," I said.

Shelly turned down Iron Maiden. "Delores can do you after she gets back from her smoke."

Of course.

I took my place in her chair. Playing with fire, now. What if I looked in the mirror and had a religious experience, found my inner Billy Ray Cyrus, and traded the bikes in for a monster truck and a trailer of Jet Skis?

Delores awaited my instructions.

"Hail Caesar," I said.

She continued to wait.

"I'll just take the same cut as my sons," I said.

I'd already spent a decade surviving Florida. That's enough redneck for one lifetime.

---

93. Joe never went the mullet route that I know of, but when he proposed to me on the top of a mountain in New Mexico I had one condition: Cut off those long thin braided strands of hair hanging off the back of your head or stay a bachelor. He also wore a little Guatemalan bag across one shoulder and was partial to a paisley vest, but I figured one thing at a time.

Chapter 14

Grumpy Old Man, Part 1

I remember when we used to sit
In the government yard in Trenchtown,
Oba—obaserving the hypocrites
As they would mingle with the good people we meet.

—Bob Marley, "No Woman No Cry"

The road between Campbell River and Port Hardy would be a hell of a place to lose a cow. That ribbon of asphalt is the only sign of the workings of man for 250 kilometers. According to unreliable sources, like Steve of Victoria and various city dwellers we spoke with along populated parts of the island, the North Country was said to be so thick with cougars, they'd be on that lost cow like hyenas tearing into a baby deer.

"Keep the boys close to you at all times."

We didn't see any animals for the first 50k, but the combination of cougar warnings and wild open country, not to mention the lack of any stores, made it a hard push so early in the ride. Weeks later, rolling through the heart of Canada, we'd laugh at these earlier fears, but at the time we were freaked out. Again, we blame Steve, who quoted some statistic about that part of the world being home to more cougars than anywhere in North America. And here we'd been thinking it was Beverly Hills.

Whatever our reasons, I found Beth and the boys a ride the rest of the way out of the wilderness, joining them a day later at what looked like the closest hotel to the ferry terminal. Port Hardy smells of rotting fish and unemployment. It's not a put-down; that's the way it was. Our waterfront hotel caught the brunt of those smells. It seemed it was also the place to congregate, so a lot of the jobless hung around telling stories and sleeping on benches. The staff at our place combated the smell with good service and smiles and gave the homeless guys out front food so they wouldn't bother the customers. Beth had already made friends of them. They let us store the bikes and gear in a conference room that no one had held a meeting in for years. The night manager, a First Nation native and a fine photographer, carried with him a sense of foreboding and resignation that was too heavy to be around for more than a few minutes.

He was riveted by our adventures but in the same breath said he could never hope to do anything like it.

"Mom calls him Eeyore, but his name is Dave. We like him, but he's a lot of work." Sometimes Quinn could sound a forty-year-old man.[94]

After a surprisingly good dinner at the sports bar, we turned in for an early evening. I'd called the ferry reservations three times, and each operator was adamant that we had to be at the terminal loading dock no later than 5 AM if we wanted a spot.

"We're on bicycles. Not motorcycles, bicycles."

The answer was the same even though I confirmed that pedestrians didn't need to check in until 7 AM.

94. Sometimes Quinn could sound like his dad.

While I repacked our gear and outfitted the bikes with lights for the unappetizing prospect of night/predawn riding, what I assumed was a wedding reception was in full swing in the basement. At times the hotel shook from a live band—drums, electric guitars, booming bass making their presence known. Good for them, the front desk assured me they'd been done by 8 PM.

The music stopped right on schedule. I put in a wake up call for 4 AM, God help us, and laid my head on the pillow.

The music cranked back up around 9 PM. Drink glasses on the nightstand shook. The walls vibrated.

"Make it stop," Beth pleaded as she went to calm Matteo.

I headed for the elevator and was joined by three other guests. Everyone's faces were full of grim resolve. I recognized two of them—a couple who'd asked about our bikes when they were checking in. He sold real estate in New Age enclaves—Sedona, Arizona, and Ashland, Oregon.

They were combining business and pleasure with a scouting mission across Canada. He'd given me his card earlier. Sacred Spaces, he called the business. She had the faraway look, dreamy smile, and monotone voice patterns of someone who'd sold flowers at the airport, or led a cult. No one was looking dreamy now.

"It's a bunch of white-trash teenagers playing their first wedding, I bet," she said. "The whole building is shaking. Believe me, they're getting a piece of my mind."

We added more members to our angry mob when the elevator stopped at the first floor. Everyone concurring that the bulk of us had to get up by 4 AM to catch a boat, and this would not do. I noticed

Dave the night manager had slipped in with the group. He'd put a stop to this nonsense.

We rounded the corner, Dreamy Lady leading the charge. I was just steps behind her. You couldn't hear yourself yell. I know because I tried to get the band's attention, then the congregation's. It wasn't a wedding but a religious meeting, a revival of Native Americans, First Nation people, as the Canadians refer to them.

I looked over to Dave, but he just stood there shaking his head. These were his people, but more importantly this was his job. I couldn't tell if he was disappointed with the situation or if that was his normal look, but he wasn't resolving it.

Dreamy Lady had gone all quiet and was slipping back off the front. I waved my hands in front of the band and the revelers out front of the music, but no one acknowledged me for a good three minutes. Finally I went over to the wall and pulled the power source.

The room fell silent.

"No disrespect intended, but do you know what time it is?" There was a clock on the wall the size of a giant serving dish. It was edging close to 9:45 PM.

"We don't feel time in the presence of the Creator," one of the congregation members said.

I shook my head.

"Well, the rest of us have to get up at 4 AM, and management told you guys to cut off at 8 PM."

A lady holding a drum said, "We thought that clock was on Daylight Saving Time?" It sounded like she was trying on the excuse for size and fit.

No one seemed to be setting down their instruments.

I took their adaptor cord and handed it to David. The room groaned. As I turned to leave someone said, "We'll pray for you."

I almost let it go. But someone had to start banging on a drum.

"Thanks, while you're at it, pray that my one-year-old gets back to sleep and hey, throw in a few words about common decency for yourselves why don't you?"

The revival was officially over.

Dreamy Lady had already headed for the elevator. She didn't hold the door for the rest of us, which seemed odd in light of recent words involving civility.

Dave rode up with me.

"Thanks," he said. "My brother's an asshole who knows exactly what time it is."

"Which one was your brother?"

"The guitar player. He pulls this crap around town every month, then he wonders why people won't give him a place to hold services."

"Hey man, I just want to get my family a good night's sleep. I wasn't trying to diss on traditions."

David looked like he hadn't slept in years.

"Just 'cause he's an Indian doesn't make him right."

"You his last hope?"

"Not anymore."

Later, on the ferry to Prince Rupert, Dreamy Lady plopped down in my booth with a view and gave me an earful.

"You should have let them play on. We've stolen so much from those people." Her face went all solemn, and she lifted her chin to the rising sun. "It's all they have left. Once again the white man comes in and takes . . ."

I didn't know where to start. I being her white man. "I thought you were ready to open up some righteous indignation when it was white-trash surf punks at their first gig. Your scorn is conditional then?"

I took a bite of a bagel while she shook her head.

"I didn't go in there with an agenda. I just wanted to get the sleep we'd paid for," I said.

She squeezed her hands together as tight as an arm wrestler. "I think you earned a black spot on your soul last night."

I couldn't argue with her on that point, but it hadn't gotten there last night. I took her husband's business card out of my pocket and slid it across the table.

"You guys flip property on land that, technically or otherwise, was once stolen from Indians. And you evoke their imagery and play on those traditions to increase profits. Your clientele are rich white folks shopping for vacation homes and spiritual fulfillment over a three-day weekend. Is that about right?"

Her face drained of color. "I don't care to get into that with you." Already backing out of the booth.

"Black spots all around," I called after her.

Beth and the boys had to dodge a scowling woman to reach our booth.

"Making friends?" Beth said.

"We won't find any deals on Sedona sweat lodges or summer homes, I can tell you that."

Beth smiled. "Real estate's never been our thing."

Chapter 15

Trying Not to Miss the Boat

To do anything truly worth doing, I must not stand back shivering and thinking of the cold and danger, but jump in with gusto and scramble through as well as I can.

—Og Mandino

Sometimes you can live several lifetimes of adventure in a few short hours. It was like that between our wake-up call and when I sat on the ship learning that I had a black spot on my soul.

We pushed into the darkness at four twenty in the morning. I imagined monks baking bread somewhere so I didn't have to think we were the only people awake at that moment. We climbed the first of several hills. It didn't feel cold anymore. That's the thing about getting on the bike and going somewhere. People who haven't tried it think the whole process is a chore, when it's really the moment right before you start that's the hardest thing you'll do all day. Getting your mind to move out of its own way. Locate the right head space and it's like calming gale-force winds until they're the soft kiss of summer breezing through the magnolias.[95]

So despite the hour, we were experiencing a catharsis, a happy-to-be-back-on-the bikes-after-days-off euphoria.

Then my headlamp died.

We rode close to each other so Beth's flasher would light the way, but it wasn't enough. I pulled over and reached for the tool of choice in most end-of-the-world emergencies. Duct tape. It wasn't pretty, but I secured a flashlight to my helmet and we were back in the game. Which was good because all the car traffic en route to the ferry from nearby hotels filled the highway.

We came to a fork. The road less traveled would put us away from traffic and, on the word of some out-of-work locals, damn near the ferry terminal.

"Let's take it," I hollered out to Beth.

A hundred yards in we knew the right thing to do was to turn

---

95. That was one of the biggest surprises of the bike trip. Once I committed myself to riding that bike every day, it was easy. It's not that people can't do it. Everyone can ride a bike. It's deciding to do it is all.

around. It wasn't lit or paved. Between the hard-packed gravel and the lack of light, I didn't feel anything close to safe with this crew. Also, the jostling on a gravel road shook the batteries in my jury-rigged head-lamp/flashlight contraption loose. I pedaled blind for a few more yards, smacking my helmet with force, hoping to whack the flashlight back into commission. It would come on and off, a poor man's strobe light.

"Retreat!" I yelled.

Beth circled back to me. We stood over handlebars paralyzed by indecision. Not only would going back to the main highway add several miles to the route, but we'd have to deal with distracted tourist traffic in the dark.

"It was a lighter dark out on the highway," Beth noted.[96]

We chose the highway, but settled on a system to keep ourselves alive. Each of us held a flashlight in our left hand. When cars came up from behind we'd hold the light at knee level, shine and wave it in an underhand early warning system. We used the car's headlights to show us the road ahead, then our own flashlights when we were alone again.

The trailer was covered in flashers, pool floaties, and flags, the boys had on their reflective safety vests, our caravan resembled an ecofriendly refugee from a gay pride parade, but I still felt practically invisible. There wasn't another ferry for two days, and it left at the same time. For once I kept Beth close enough to hear her breathing.

The flat tire was so unexpected that I refused to believe it at first. When you're focusing on cars in front and behind you, road debris that's easily avoidable in the light of day goes undetected at night. We

96. Not by much but a dirt road of darkness, I mean complete darkness, seemed like a bad call.

that's easily avoidable in the light of day goes undetected at night. We were about half a mile from the terminal. I could see massive floodlights in the distance.

It was quarter to five. I hoped the ferry boat company was happy. They'd put my family's lives on the line.[97]

"Baby, ride on and hold our spot. I'm gonna push and coast and limp us in." If I tried to do a quick change or patch in the dark we could be there indefinitely.

"Boys, keep shining your lights at the cars before they get up on us. And I want you to walk on the inside, keeping the bike between you and the grass."

I watched Beth's little Tinkerbell light wave and flash in the dark ahead of us. She was making good time. Every time a car passed her I let out a sigh of relief. I picked up the pace as much as I dared, then backed off so the boys didn't stumble into the grass and wind up in a ditch.

Once we pushed the bike up the last hill, I chanced riding the wounded beast on the flats. We rolled up to the waiting area just before 5 AM.

No one was there to greet us. No one waved us into a certain lane. Beth flashed her light at us and we came over.

At the ticket counter the woman said I must have misunderstood. Bicyclists were counted with the pedestrians and didn't need to be here until 7 AM.

---

97. I'm telling you, anger should be the new energy drink. I was so pissed at the ferry company then that I could have pedaled across water just to give them a piece of my mind.

Beth was near tears. The boys were exhausted from the whole ordeal. That's when I asked to speak to the dock manager.

"Here are the names and employee numbers of the three different
people who told us to be here by 5 AM. I wanted to come later but they
said it was 5 AM or they'd drop our reservation." I shook my head. "You
put my family in harm's way."

After a few phone calls, the manager morphed into an entirely different guy. We were offered coffee and doughnuts and apologies. "The
people you spoke with aren't even at this location. It's a call center in
Quebec."

All we wanted was to see the sunrise from the deck of a ship headed
north through whale country.

"I'd like our tickets comped," Beth announced, holding a sleepy
Matteo. He was giving the stink eye to anyone in uniform. I liked this
new Beth. Put her little cubs in jeopardy you'd face the consequences.
The road makes you bold.

The manager excused himself, never to return.

An ensign who'd been listening to the whole thing stepped up. "I
rode my bike from Vancouver to San Diego when I was in college."
He looked off in the distance for a few seconds, somewhere back on
that trip, no doubt.

"Good luck getting a dime out of these guys, but see me when you
get on board and we'll make it right despite 'em, eh?"[98]

Our mood improved. I hadn't sweat that much before 5 AM in

---

98. He got us a tour of the wheelhouse and the captain apologized about the mixup
and let the boys steer the ship for a bit. Which I thought was a bit of a risk, considering my boys.

years, and it actually felt good, plus we were still alive as the morning light began to reveal amazing country—which we were about to see more of from the deck of a ship.

When it was time to load on, our ensign, true to his word, was looking out for us. He waved us through first. We pedaled past a fleet of waiting cars like we were lead off float at a Mardi Gras parade.

"When do we get back on the bikes?"

We were watching whales breach off the boat's bow on a two-day sail to Prince Rupert, after three full weeks on tour. In a setting like this could she really be thinking about the ride?

"You've been a real sport about everything," I said, "but you don't have to mock me."

Here's the thing: She wasn't.[99] Amazing as the boat ride had been, Beth was experiencing cycling withdrawals. She wanted back on the bike, the good sore felt right before you start another day. Then it leaving your body with each pedal stroke. The wondering if you had another day in you, then realizing you do. The need for speed and movement and freedom. The simple purpose of each day.

I hold my wife close as the sun sets behind us. Except for the child strapped to her back and the other two spitting off the bow, it could have been our honeymoon. Knowing how Beth felt about biking now certainly made me as happy as a newlywed.

"Soon, baby. We've got the rest of Canada to go yet."

---

99. Joe talks about my transformation a lot. But during that downtime in Port Hardy and on the boat, I realized how much I missed bike touring. I'll mock him any chance I get, but he'd given me something real with this bike touring.

PART 3

Joe and Beth:
The Greatest Love Story Ever Told (This Week)

Mom

Mom never learned how to ride a bike. As evidence, she produces a photo of herself sitting beside her older sister—a busy street in Greece makes up the backdrop—arm bandaged, smile tentative.

"I wrecked earlier that afternoon and I haven't been on a bike since." She says this with a certain amount of satisfaction.

Faith in her abilities fell short that day. Which is not Mom's MO. Raised by hardhearted nuns in a European boarding school, she faced them down without flinching, took her licks, raised hell, rose above, became a ballerina, a damn good one, with her own studio in New York City, taught school in Harlem, held a family of four children together despite what should have been debilitating rheumatoid arthritis, created a safe, loving, secret garden of a childhood for us, when it must have been a daily dogfight to get her joints to fall in line, pulled her husband out of emotional and financial crises along the way, and made him get back on the metaphoric bicycle more than once.

But when it came to pedaling a two-wheeler again, she walked away without regret.

"Which is why I get such a kick out of the fact that you're the Metal Cowboy," she says. "I ride through you."

Even at seventy, bent by her long dance with disease, she keeps a fire burning in her eyes most days. Losing my father threatened to grind her spirit to dust, but somehow she shouldered it. Put it on and carried it.

She would have made a hell of a cyclist.

Chapter 16

A Beautiful Wreck

A man content to go to heaven alone will never go to heaven.
—Boethius

History will forget about most of us. If you're not a narcissist, thief, power monger, or exhibitionist, you'll have trouble making it into the books. I've been all these things at one time, but on such a petty scale it only shames me in my quieter moments, not on the front pages. Here's the thing, though: History, the one that's written down, is the long con. It's dinner and one hell of a show, but it's not what actually happened. For that, you had to have been there.

Besides, the only history worth learning are those moments when we connect with each other, or try to. Making some sense out of the universe by holding a living, breathing piece of it in your hands.

That's when it gets messy.

Those first lazy evenings under the hoodoos and pinnacles, we hiked around Bryce Canyon by moonlight and talked about anything that came into our heads.[100]

Hidden up there in a not-so-mythical fortress of solitude with real geological mysteries eight thousand feet above sea level, Beth made me feel authentic for maybe the first time in my life. No small feat for a perpetually recovering white man. I stopped rolling my *r*'s when pronouncing *Nicaragua,* embraced my pop-culture roots, and exposed my inner Florida redneck upbringing, and Beth didn't look at me like I was from another planet. We had a good laugh at our earnestness. In spite of that we pledged over a list of our favorite movie titles and best birthday memories, that we'd try to make a difference in this world, and, failing that, to never be cruel.[101]

100. I don't remember how far we walked, I remember we got into my truck and drove up to a lookout point to see the moon rise over Alligator Rock. I'll give it to Joe, though. He had to push the truck out of a ditch to get us started, and I didn't help matters by putting it in third gear while he strained against a couple thousand pounds of Toyota. He must have known I was going to be a project right from the beginning.
101. Mostly I remember a lot of discussions about Ann Rice's vampire books, seeing a full harvest moon rise and the sun set at the same time, and that Joe was the nicest of a parade of horny men who tried to "talk" to me across the Desert Southwest. What a freak show the trip brought out. I'm lucky to be alive. Joe acknowledged this when he gave me a can of Mace and told me they all weren't bark with no bite. He

Then it was over, my time out of mind with an amazing person, and then just me again, racing back to sea level, weaving and leaning through the curves, doing reckless things on a bicycle because that's what a young man does when he's in love for the first time.[102]

I didn't know it as love, not yet. I thought maybe it was food poisoning. The pit of my stomach churning, causing hunger and pain at the same time. And weak, a bone weariness down to my soul. I'd never had my strength desert me on the inside. After Bryce, I could still pedal a hundred miles into a headwind, but inside I was tissue paper. When I rolled into Zion National Park the hole had shifted from my gut to my heart, where it stayed, only to bloat further out with every mile. I missed this winsome young woman and there was nothing I could do about it. The chaos playing on my broken thoughts reminded me of the time, as a teenager, Clark and I got lost at sea.[103]

All my adventures by bike had brought me close to larger-than-life characters: lunatics, visionaries, cons, and vagabond kings. And when

also said something about being careful if I ever tested it because wind direction can be a bit tricky—"breezes in the desert can be a fickle bastard" were his exact words. Then he touched his sunburned face and laughed a slightly crazy laugh. He's always cracking himself up, which you learn to live with because, while some of it's for his own amusement and the peanut gallery in his head, the rest is actually funny, like this-guy-should-have-his-own-late-night-talk-show funny. People ask me what it's like living with the Metal Cowboy. I tell them I don't know but the truth about living with Joe, it's never boring. Tiresome sometimes, but I'm never bored. I'm just saying, most marriages get boring before all the rice has fallen from the gown. Not ours. A three-ring circus and sometimes crashing into a ditch but even for that I'm grateful, really. Oh, and I felt comfortable right off when I was with him.

102. News flash, he wasn't that young. I was nineteen, he was around twenty-five. But guys take a lot longer to grow up, so it was just about even.

103. Joe loves his nautical references. Stop him if he breaks into a sea chantey. BTW, he was never lost at sea. He and his buddy were caught in a storm for about twenty minutes in the Gulf of Mexico and got a little turned around. They made it home by dinner. Next he'll be writing about an albatross and some big fish and want to buy a place in Key West.

those times together ended, I felt loss and longing, sure, but this was different. This was an unwieldy thing I didn't know where to put. I just knew that I'd fight you if you tried to take the memory of her from me.[104]

Since I was a young man rather than a smart one, the dots took a while to connect. We'll talk about nothing of importance with intensity. And go on for years like that, when what we need has already walked into our lives.

A week into this heartache, I decided to treat it with strong medicine: a Scorsese[105] movie. And not just any film, *Goodfellas*. A Tuesday matinee in small-town New Mexico. With the bike secured out front, I found myself alone with a box of popcorn and those crazy eyes of Ray Liotta for two solid hours. Gritty waves of street justice and pistol-whipped reality would set me right. Put me back on the good foot—the one that says we're born alone, die alone, and remain hopelessly confused in between.[106]

104. And he's felt this way for me ever since. Even when I didn't think I was worth fighting for anymore.
105. Embarrassing footnote about the time Joe met Martin Scorsese. Yes, the director of *Goodfellas*. A few years after sitting in that theater, Joe was sitting across from *Raging Bull*'s maker. He'd taken a job as the arts and entertainment editor of a small, undistinguished daily newspaper. Since it was the only news source of record for fifteen thousand square miles, basically the rest of New Mexico below Albuquerque, he landed interviews well above his professional station. As he puts it, "What always started with good intentions and painstakingly prepared research would devolve into some of the most starstruck questions of stupidity one human being has ever asked another. Scorsese was making a western in rural New Mexico. The HiLo Country. I brought the diminutive man of multiple Academy Award nominations to a complete stop, blindsiding him in the middle of a cloudless afternoon, with this gem: 'Emotionally speaking, how do you prepare to off a made man?' His wild hand gesturing ceased, those darting eyes held mine the way one tracks a big, potentially lethal animal. 'You do realize that all this is make-believe?' I'd love to tell you that was the last dumb question I ever asked an interviewee." Another from Joe's greatest hits that comes to mind: the time he asked Keanu Reeves what it felt like to act.

It did not take. Though I found myself swearing with bravado in an Italian accent along desolate stretches of New Mexico's dusty back roads, which, as it happens, is most of them.

I pedaled under the weight of a heavy heart, all the way to a wilderness ranger job at the Gila Cliff Dwellings. *Job* is too strong a word for what I would be doing for the federal government that season. They gave me a "cabin" aka single-wide trailer, a cool seventeen dollars a day, ten of which went unspent, and all the untamed wilderness I could handle, hike, swim, or cover by horseback. In return, I manned a collection of thirteen-hundred-year-old dwellings tucked high in the cliffs above the middle fork of the Gila River. I learned enough about the local archaeology, history, flora, and fauna to answer tourists' questions, or fake it with conviction, but mostly I watched a red fox sun itself in the morning light, chopped wood for the stove some afternoons, and used the balance of my days learning to be quiet with myself. Which, for anyone who knows me, is quite the herculean task.

I'd barely inspected my living quarters when heartache forced me out-of-doors again. Since the "job" didn't officially start for another five days, I borrowed a pack, a map, and all the supplies I could forage from the fire crew bunkhouse—gorp, some dried foods, and a harmonica.[107]

Thousands of miles of roadless wilderness might just do what

106. Freaky coincidence moment: While Joe was sharing a few hours in the dark with crazy-eyed Ray, I was also in New Mexico, seeing the very same movie with my mother. Who, in her version of a pep talk, used to give me the "You're born alone, you die alone" speech. Only hers ended with "so in the meantime get me some coffee."
107. Joe—I don't know how to play but I thought it might be a good time to take it up.

Scorsese couldn't. That, or I'd get eaten by a big cat. Either way, pain gone, weight lifted, problem solved.

Five days later I stumbled out of the backcountry a righted ship. The Gila wilderness is like few places on earth. Five distinct ecozones ranging from high desert to alpine, it dwarfed me with its enormity, swallowing my worries and burdens. I allowed the ponderosa pines, alligator junipers, and azure blue skies of late October to slowly draw out the primal parts of me buried too long under suburban parking lots, petty compromises, and trips to the mall. I drank directly from streams and stopped setting up my tent altogether.[108]

The ranger caught me coming out at the bridge separating the wilderness boundary from the visitor's center parking lot. I stood there, between two worlds. At that moment I thought I might have the courage to choose the wild over society forever.

That autumn, single, with scant possessions and no one waiting up for me anywhere, was the closest I've ever come to pulling my own *Into the Wild.*

I smelled like a week of campfires when he handed me two pink slips of paper, the ones people wrote phone messages on before we started allowing round-the-clock cellular intrusion into our days.

"You're a popular guy."

I almost pocketed the papers, assuming they were from my mother. Not sending word of my safe arrival from the Canadian border was bound to have repercussions. While I'd conditioned my family to ex-

---

108. He still doesn't set up his tent much of the time. Let's not read too much Ed Abbey into the process, though. I think it's sloth commingled with a general lack of concern for his safety and exhaustion. When Joe shuts down it's like sleeping beside a mindless caveman.

pect me to emerge from under a rock after the end of the world, mothers will worry.

Then a winsome young woman from the high-mountain fortress flashed through my thoughts. I actually spoke Beth's name out loud and buckled slightly as all the weight I'd shed in the woods returned. It wasn't a burden anymore. I knew what I was carrying and I wanted to carry it as long as it took to be together.[109]

The first note read, "Beth from Bryce, arriving Saturday @ 2."

What's a man look like when he realizes he's about to get everything he wants? Not unlike a pig on an ice rink doing an awkward little herky jig with enough force to shake a bridge. The ranger threw a look of concern over his shoulder on the way back to his truck. If not for me, then for his bridge. Or it might have been the whooping sounds coming out of me. A spastic cheerleader in full beard suffering the throes of a grand mal seizure. Hell, I'd have looked, too. Technically, I was still in the wilderness, which meant I could do damn near anything I wanted. Freedom of expression on public lands. What a country.[110, 111, 112]

Spent and a little dizzy, I leaned against the railing. Using formidable detective skills honed through marathon viewings of *The Rockford Files,* I could assume Beth felt something between us. Look, people

109. He can be sweet. I'm not sure I believe it. Did your legs really buckle? Show me.
110. The first time I thought of Joe as anything more than a friend was when he stepped out of the Forest Service bunkhouse, clean-shaven and sporting a light blue J. Crew sweater. Thank God I wasn't there for the bearded cheerleader routine. No longer looking like a Scandinavian version of Sasquatch.
111. I thought of myself something akin to a manly-smelling honey bear.
112. Not so much honey bear, just smelly. See, some men can pull off the full-on Jeremiah Johnson look. Not my Boo. He's a fleece-and-goatee guy all the way. And if he's gonna dance, make sure it's not too complicated . . . reggae's a good call.

don't drive to the middle of nowhere just for the scenery.

One look in any direction shot holes through that crackerjack detective work. Fifty-two thousand people drove to the middle of that specific nowhere each year. I'd just read that very statistic in the cliff dwelling visitor's guide. Also, didn't she say she was on a national parks greatest hits of the Southwest tour?[113]

Perhaps the second pink slip would be a subtle clue to Beth's real feelings. "PS I love you with the force of Pamplona bulls running those narrow streets of Pamplona," that sort of thing. I pulled it from my pocket, unwrapped it like it was the golden ticket, then stared at it long and hard, the way one might study a birthday party goody bag that turns out to be filled with wet catshit.

"Alicia from the science museum, arriving Saturday @ 2."

I look up to see the ranger still standing between the door and cab of his truck. His grin and head shake say it all.

I try to recall how many days I think I've been in the woods.

"Hey, what time is it?" I yell.

But he's already gunning the engine out of the lot.

There's a wall clock in the visitor's station, but the building's locked and I haven't been issued keys yet. I stand at the sliding door straining past the reflective glass to see the important parts of clock around the pipe of the woodstove and the horns of a stuffed elk.

Who's Alicia you ask?[114]

113. After exactly eleven days and six hours with my mother in her northern New Mexico one-room adobe house—she was on one of her wacky dietary-restrictive healing phases of the moon—I frantically flipped through my address book and Joe's distinctive all-caps, block-letters handwriting jumped out at me. There's a teeny, tiny chance that I might have been looking for it.
114. Yeah, let's hear him talk his way out of this one.

Do we have to get into that right now? I'm doing advanced geometry problems here, with what's left of an elk and the long division end of a woodstove.

Fine. During a less-than-triumphant return to Florida I may have made a bit of a mess out of my life and a few others. In my experience cracking the border of the Sunshine State as anything more than a tourist is a boxload of mistakes in the making. But then I spent fifteen of my formative years there, so I'm biased and slightly cynical on the place.

Besides, Jim Rockford wouldn't want to know about the woman. He'd ask, "What science museum?" Of course I want to talk about that job only slightly more than I want to reminisce about Alicia. Did I mention my return to Florida was something of a mixed bag?[115]

I was assigned to the museum during a statewide cleanup day. We pulled a few tons of junk out of a sandhill habitat behind the building. Alicia was the museum's program director running the cleanup.

I kept pointing out all the wildlife and plants they had on the forty acres, and by the end of the afternoon Alicia had convinced me to come work for them.

Our first task was to turn the back forty acres of sandhill habitat— a jungle for palms, thick understory, and Spanish moss—into an interactive classroom and ecofriendly exhibit. Had I known then what I know now, I would have told the board of directors that the best thing

115. Guest Footnote by Jim Rockford—If I were a real person and not a character played by the esteemed James Garner I would tell you that I don't give a rat's ass about a science museum. I want to know about the girl. Let's hear it.

we could do for the public's education and the environment in general was to leave it the hell alone. In my experience, people don't like to hear that.

It feels too much like releasing manifest destiny on its own recognizance without giving it the old college try. In my defense, I wanted a meaningful job, something that didn't involve hair nets and Happy Meals. Writing the next great American novel while saving habitat and educating youth about how and why we should felt like an honest way to pay the bills. As an added benefit it kept my dad from asking if I needed to borrow any money and if I'd found myself yet.

Alicia and I worked together in close quarters that first month. The state of Florida was giving away grant money to protect habitat while developing educational opportunities on it. We ordered in food, brainstormed, got punchy in the wee hours cooking up wild ideas. We worked nearly round the clock the final week to beat the submission deadline. By the time the grant went into the mail we had become pals.

All that time together allowed us to come up with something we dubbed the global mailbox trail. There would be globe-shaped structures with a mailbox enveloped within, on posts stationed throughout the forty acres. Each would have activities stored inside, pertaining to that specific part of the habitat. We also designed a butterfly garden and an orienteering course with destinations to different biology lessons and visual wonders. All of this came with a strong message of preservation, bordering on indictment of most of man's actions within modern society. What the hell, go big, we thought, cause as much trouble as we could until they throw you to the curb.[116, 117]

Instead of being shown the door, we got the grant. It was Friday afternoon near quitting time. A rather dangerous hour to get good news. On the way out the door, we picked up employees like party favors, each of them looking for any excuse to be loud and get lit.

The weekend was made official when, in the museum parking lot, someone turned up the bass to Rusted Root on a car stereo and passed around a bottle of Southern Comfort.

By Saturday morning I'd done things with my supervisor that could not be taken back. Having no idea what to do next, I told Alicia I'd scheduled a bicycle ride with an old friend for that morning and fled the premises.

I nearly tore the skin from my legs, as hard as I spun them that morning. What we refer to as a pore-cleaner ride on account of how much sweat runs out of you. Back then it was how I saw clear to where I wanted to go in my life; failing that, it helped me locate some peace within the helplessness. Years later, it's still cheap, effective therapy.

Thank God no one's made a bike that can go fast enough to outpace life's problems. Or found a road long enough to lose 'em. That'd be a cheat that I'd be too weak to resist. Like shuttling by car to the top of a mountain for the downhill tuck and go, or sitting to a plate

116. Beth—Ahh those #$%& globes. The global trail dream of Joe's followed us around for years. It got to the point where we toured plastic factories outside El Paso, Texas. This is where we learned that it would take a financial outlay of one hundred thousand dollars just to create the molds. That was the end of that, thank you Jesus.
117. Joe—What I didn't take into account was that a museum that makes exhibits has its own fabrication equipment. A guy on a bicycle does not know the first thing about large-scale manufacturing. Which is just as well, because, in hindsight, putting plastic globes in natural settings was just adding to the problem—no matter how much education I thought it would bring to the masses.

crowded with southern BBQ, pulled pork, hushpuppies, and sides when you haven't earned it with real labor.

My best rides give me enough momentum to turn into my troubles and face down the day, nothing more.

Besides, it's a hell of a thing to hang over your handlebars tasting parts of your insides sitting up around your tonsils. In those moments, everything else seems small and manageable.

She did not view the significance of the evening's events in the same light. The candles at dinner being the first sign. Damn it. And I was really grooving on the museum job. Did I mention that I was down to my last twenty when I took it? Also, that I was hunting about for a place to live? My bro's couch was more a port of call than a home stand.

I should have walked away. Instead, I drank up and let future Joe figure it out. From there it got complicated and strange, but really pretty simple and familiar to anyone who's spent any time living on their own. Alternatively, those who still live at home but watch a lot of daytime TV.

My brother said I could keep my stuff at his condo. This time he even promised he might not sell it. Tim and Alicia lived in the same complex. I kept a spot on the couch made up like I was living with Tim, but I was in "trouble" if I didn't spend most of the time at Alicia's. Tim didn't like that we were together and made it clear. Alicia's roommate Bonnie, an evangelical Christian, didn't like it that anyone was together without a wedding ring, and made it clear. I agreed with both of them but couldn't bring myself to leave, not while the museum project was going so well. Another thing was Bonnie's hit list of all the Robbie Robertson music. After I informed her that he'd played Woodstock, she stomped her foot and squeezed her eyes shut, trying to exorcise the echoes of his music from the building. When I added, out of cruelty, that I thought he might have written some of the melodies for *Jesus Christ Superstar* her throat started to close up. She ran to her part of the house and tried blasting the musical stylings of John Tesh. Much like a bomb shelter, though, The Tesh is blastproof.

The whole thing was wrong on so many levels, not only the Tesh parts. More flustered than at any time since the summer months following my high school graduation, I opened my first bank account in years and simply stopped trying to come clean with Alicia. She'd done nothing to deserve this relationship of convenience. While I was off hiking in the Smokey Mountains with her and wondering where my actually soul mate might be, Tim was back home selling off some of my best stuff just to prove a point.

Confronted with my failures of character, I soldiered on for a while longer. I ended it in a children's playground one Friday afternoon. Me on the seesaw, Alicia in a swing across the way. We were supposed to go eat crawfish and listen to blues, but I took her there instead.

"I shouldn't have met your folks."

This confused her. "'Cause it was Passover? They don't care you're not Jewish."

"'Cause . . . I know this isn't going anywhere." Yes, I'd said it out loud. I needed to complete the motion or spend more days sick over the pretender I'd become. To feel better I'd have to cut my way out of there. A cad's retreat is straight through the heart with the sharpest words he can find.

"Did you ever feel something?" Her voice fighting to hold together.

I didn't look up, which was worse than any lies my body had told in the dark. She was still on the swing when I left. Not even a decent cad.

To her credit, we continued to work well together into April. What I didn't know was that Alicia was telling people, and herself, that we were fine.

While trouble brewed under the surface on that front, our back-lot museum habitat project blew up in my face.

I was coming off the high of introducing Al Gore at one of the largest Earth Day events in the country. This was Gore when he was still a mild-mannered senator from a southern state, trying to get folks to buy the audacious theory that the world was heating up and there was no technological silver bullet to beat the rap on this one. It was the twentieth anniversary of Earth Day; still, who would have thought that backward Florida could pull together that many concerned souls standing near the Hillsboro River in the April sunshine. I somehow found myself master of ceremonies, working the crowd into a frenzy about recycling, simple living, and green solutions. Thousands of folks stayed silent while a stocky politician, the only man in a suit for three counties, told them in wooden but no uncertain terms that they were f-ing things up but good with nearly every choice they made each waking moment of their consumption-gone-wild lives.

He came at them hard, then harder. Think *Braveheart* minus the accent and kilt.

It was something to see.

I think people might have heard his message, too. They were ready for it. After the mockery that passed for civilization in the 1980s, leg warmers and parachute pants alone caused so many to pause and ponder.

Only trouble was, the distinguished gentleman from Tennessee was followed by the owner of The Body Shop, sporting a miniskirt, a British accent, and a living, breathing chimpanzee rescued from a testing facility. The monkey did Gore in. It joined her on stage, even doing a few backflips while she spoke. And though they had the foresight not to dress it in overalls or alligator shirts, the chimp had been provided his own booth off to the side of the stage where he conducted on-site makeovers. Yes, the monkey was actually applying cruelty-free Body Shop cosmetics to volunteers called up from the crowd; brushing on mascara and rubbing lotions into the backs of sweaty Floridians with no end in sight.

A different form of animal cruelty if you ask me.

Gore's five-alarm fire speech never had a chance. It found a lot of applause at the time, but the monkey made the papers.[118]

A lot of folks might have been watching the monkey, but I was hanging on the future vice president's every got-damned word.

So when later that week the museum director and his board decided that a prudent use of twenty of our forty-acre habitat behind the museum would be a parking lot to accommodate a thirty-million-dollar IMAX theater, I stormed into a closed session with heaps of Gore-inspired righteous indignation and a fully grown gopher tortoise.

Technically, it was illegal to remove a gopher tortoise from its habi-

118. Years later, Al would lose another important battle in Florida to an oil man of privilege nicknamed Curious George.

tat, but considering the discussion was whether to pave over much of said reptile's home turf, I decided exceptions could be made.[119]

This is how the world works. One cheeky monkey trumps dire warnings of global warming, but a slow-moving tortoise does nothing to impede progress when thirty million dollars of municipally bonded funds and private capital are on the line.

"No, we don't see this as violating the parameters of the grant you wrote," said the museum's director said. He substituted efficiency in all things for wisdom in any. "The turtle's holes are on the east end of the property. We'll simply move the butterfly cages and shift the global trail to make room for our patrons' parking needs."

I set the tortoise loose atop an expensive teak conference table. Its nails made a horrible racket scraping against the wood, as it tried to gain some traction. Had none of these people read the portion of the grant outlining complete-system ecology? I scanned the room and I decided to reason with them in their own language.

"Anyone thought about a parking garage? Up instead of out with all that pavement? Everyone gets to keep their homes."

At an additional four dollars per square foot, no one had thought about it for long. I held up the tortoise. It kept flapping its legs at the open air, a windup toy taken out of play. What we had was a Mexican standoff, except I'd pulled a tortoise and they'd drawn double barrels of "progress." I shot anyway.

---

119. I can just see him with that tortoise. When I met Joe he was full of conviction—about how we were wrecking the planet because everyone took more than they needed. I loved that beneath his bohemian look was a guy who believed in what he was saying. He still does, even after life has forced him to make certain choices and compromises.

"You do know the tortoise's back door is located where you want to put the bus parking!" My voice too loud even for a carpeted room.

A board member, the banker partnering on the IMAX project doing his time in the community service trenches—translation, watching his investment—dropped the campaign trail grin.

"I've been told you're something of a writer. This would be an excellent institution to continue lending your talents to, but you'll need to learn which battles are worth fighting . . . and who's on your side."

I held his stare for longer than was polite.

If, in that moment, I could have caught the sandhill crane that nested in an oak tree on the west side of the property, I would have set it loose in the room, squawking, feathers flying, then I would have rooted for its sharp beak to put out an eye or two in the ensuing chaos. Mine even.

All was tense silence, save for the gentle flapping of tortoise legs—I thought of them as the sound of unanswered prayers in the climate-controlled wind.

The director raised his hands in mock surrender. "No one wants to hurt the turtle," he said. "You'll see."

Before leaving, I jabbed the docile creature in the general direction of the suits, ending with the director.

Him, I offered a tight, sad smile.

"No, you'll see." Even to me that sounded like someone who might come back and burn the place down.

I turned to leave, but thought better of it. The director held a master's degree in zoology. I jabbed the reptile once more in his direction.

"And quit calling it a turtle. It's a tortoise, you f-wit."

❧

My affairs seemed in order. I'd closed the short-lived bank account, converted seven grand, "blood money" as I now referred to it, into traveler's checks, removed a floppy disk containing all traces of the curriculum, building specs, and materials to complete our projects. All I needed was a postage stamp to mail a whistleblower letter to the governor's office in charge of funding and my work would be done. I put the letter and the comically large floppy disk—it was the size of a Chubby Checker 45 from the 1950s—into my bike bag and pedaled down to the Greyhound station.

Yet another heroic departure from my hometown.

My bus didn't leave for another hour. Since I hadn't paid rent during the three months I'd spent mucking about in Alicia's life, I felt I owed her something. Not money of course. No self-righteous twenty-five-year-old male brain is wired that way. It never crossed my mind to put a wad of cash in an envelope with a short note and no forwarding address.

Pride goes before a fall. My experience is that men in their twenties consist almost entirely of pride, wound around a ball of sports trivia, held in place with some navel lint.

I called her at work, reenacting the drama in the boardroom with sound effects and voices and hand gestures, even though she couldn't see any of them. With that bit of self-aggrandizing fun behind us, I said I was out of there. Dropping off the grid for a while. Maybe "bike down the spine of the Rockies" was vague. Let them try to build their global trail without the owner's manual. It was going straight to the governor's with my tell-all letter.

"I'm sorry it didn't work between us," I whispered into the phone, because whispering the final kiss-off made it seem, to me, somehow less cruel. I didn't mention that I had the disk and a letter penned to the governor in my saddlebag. She didn't mention that the board of directors was laughing at me, since half of them sat on the governor's committee funding the project.

She sounded calm and together. Not even a casual inquiry as to what I was planning next.

Tom Petty's "Freefalling" played over the terminal sound system. I boarded the bus that afternoon feeling light and uncaged.

Three months and six thousand miles later. I couldn't say I understood why Alicia was about to pull into the middle of nowhere, and at the very moment Beth from Bryce was wheeling in also.

How had she found me?

But it did confirm one thing: I still hadn't found a road long enough to leave life's loose ends behind . . .

And something else. I've never been sure if I believe in karma, but I think it was about to kick my ass.

Had I really brought this soap opera to the woods? The elk head was too damn big to see around, so I gave up on clock-watching and wandered back to the bridge to await my fate. On the upside, dime store drama had never played in such a breathtaking setting. The alders up through the canyon were in full color for the autumn turn, and the creek that quenched the thirsts of a civilization for thousands of years still ran strong and steady. That was something. I focused on it while I waited.

Beth's truck was unmistakable as it pulled up and bucked to a stop. Her driving had only improved slightly since that first afternoon when I pushed her truck out of a ditch.[120]

Any thoughts I might have entertained about dodging my troubles and those of a corrupted world by wandering into the woods, never to be heard from again, well, those were dashed in stunning fashion when she eased out of the cab.

Forget her scuffed cowboy boots or hand-cut jeans shorts, the worn-in-all-the-right-places tank top, or strawberry-blond hair spilling over tanned shoulders in the September sun,[121] I couldn't look directly into or completely away from her eyes. Biology working overtime for sure, but also I wanted to get to know the person she didn't show the world, if she'd give me a chance . . . And I'd mocked love songs throughout my youth by singing AC/DC choruses whenever Paul McCartney worked himself into a full-blown whine.

I wanted Beth more than any bike adventure, any ideals about rugged independence . . . any gopher tortoise habitat. But it wouldn't happen if I turned my back on the workings of man, or come clean about another, possibly armed, probably vengeful woman arriving momentarily.

We held each other just a few seconds longer than friends do. Or I didn't let go when I should have. Either way I felt the embrace had

---

120. I got two speeding tickets and got trapped in Mexico for several hours because I didn't know how to do a tight three-point turn to get me out of the line at the border crossing.

121. I looked all right but Joe's going a little overboard. I wonder where the cowboy boots went. I loved those things. A friend of ours sank clips into a pair of her boots so she can pedal around in them. I might like to try that.

promise. I glanced over my shoulder. Thankfully, the parking lot was still empty.

I had this one chance.

A tour of the cliff dwellings at the hands of a less-than-professional guide leaving immediately—this seemed like the right course of action. Within a hundred yards we'd fallen into the easy conversation of people who have known each other for years, a weekend yard party feel, festive and unforced. In a few minutes I lost all impulse control, taking Beth's hand as we passed through the dwellings, an old couple on vacation. It felt tender rather than forward. We'd time-traveled to the end of decades together and we were still holding hands. For Beth's part, she didn't let go.

With the fox not far away and a family of deer munching understory on the canyon plateau across from the dwellings, we'd stumbled onto the set of Disney's Bambi. I considered picking her some purple lupines, tucking them gently into her hair, but it's illegal to pick any flora or fauna on national monument grounds.

I swallowed hard.

"I have all these feelings for you, and it's confusing as hell, but if you feel anything along the same lines I'd really like to spend some time together and see where it leads."

When she smiled, Beth's face came alive. It does to this day.

She reached down, picked a handful of contraband purple lupines,[122] oblivious to her felonious act, and told me there was something going on for her, too.

---

122. I did not pick lupines. Under his spell of love or not, I know my wildflowers.

Everything in the universe changed in that moment. Ridiculous, I know, but I swear somewhere black holes released light and time continuums course-corrected. I had a chance, a real shot of making a life, nothing colossal or stately, but something authentic . . . as long as I told the truth.

"But here's the thing . . . ," I said.

Beth squinted. Probably thinking, *Married? Bike-accident-related impotence? Commitment phobia?*[123]

"There's a woman about to pull into the parking lot down there." I rubbed my face hard, defeated but determined to see my absurd speech through.

"And you have no reason to believe me on this, but here's the truth. I had a short unnecessary thing with her back in Florida. It ended before it started really. My fault, on account of poor judgment, general stupidity, and a desire to avoid confrontation . . ."

It sounded even more ridiculous out loud then it had in my head.

"Anyway, I just found out she's on her way here. God knows, I'm a little frightened mulling over why she's driven a car with suspect brakes and oil issues three thousand miles or how she found me . . ." I ran out of verbal runway at that point so I just pulled the pink slips from my pockets and handed them over like hall passes or something my mother had given me to show the teacher to clear everything up.

Beth looked them over.

A testament to her feelings for me that my future wife didn't feed the phone messages to the little red fox and grind her clutch right out

123. Actually, I was wondering why there's always a "but" . . .

of there.[124]

We took our time on the walk back.

Alicia stepped onto the bridge just as we reached it.

"Why don't you check out the park headquarters bookstore. I'll try to clear this up." I gave Beth's hand a quick squeeze. No squeeze back, but a smile.

"And if you want to pat her down for firearms on your way by, that'd be all right with me."

The women passed each other. Alicia's face darkened a little, or maybe I was just imagining.

We took the same walk up the canyon, but the house party vibe was gone. The fox and family of deer had vacated the premises. Animals are the first to detect when a destructive force of nature is about to roll in.

"All we needed was a geographic change," Alicia began with. "The relationship was too complicated as your supervisor. The politics of the museum were a nightmare. Don't get me started. None of that was right for us."

Holy crap, she'd quit her job.

This was no fender bender. I'd wrecked the thing proper. If Alicia were a hotel room then I was Keith Richards after a night of drinking and drugs, staggering between the furniture, breaking the expensive shit with a spastic's reeling accuracy.

Repeatedly shaking my head didn't seem to be working, so I added

124. It was a windy, two-hour drive back to town, and I'd only just surfaced my feelings for Joe when he took my hand. Still smelling like soot, Joe hadn't shaved that pitiful white-boy attempt at a beard yet, so I decided to stay put, see how he cleaned up, and let this thing play itself out. Who knew, he might even have been telling the truth about the "other woman."

some words.

"But we'd decided to be friends long before I left," I said in a sooth-ing tone, one reserved for use by dedicated nurses on the late shift.

She frowned. "Then what was that weekend before you took off all about?"

Oh, right . . .

Saying that it was my way of letting her down gently wasn't going to fly, except to establish me as a bigger a-hole than I was only now starting to realize myself to be. Hey, I'm that guy. It's a bracing place to find yourself. Go ahead, roll your eyes, I'll wait for everyone who has-n't made a mess of someone else's life.

I thought about cradling my head in my hands, but that felt too country-music-song for my tastes.

Instead, I talked in the language of a TV therapist, using the phrases *getting beyond, moving forward, pushing past this,* and finding some *mu-tual closure.* In other words, the language of a coward.

I ended with "I'm truly sorry you drove all this way for nothing." Weak, but better than cradling my head.

She stepped back to get a better look at me.

"I'm not going anywhere," she said. "I got the same job you did, for the whole winter." I'd left the magazine *Helping Out in the Outdoors* in her office trash can, with the job description and phone numbers cir-cled. Jim Rockford would have pimp-slapped me for that move. Alicia even told the park service we were engaged, so they signed her up, slot-ting us in the same cabin. Which still didn't make up for sleeping with her the week before I left, but it was a step in the right direction.

Her bombshell forced me to take a seat on a primitive, hand-carved bench marked DO NOT SIT in bland government signage colors. Only moments earlier, I'd invited Beth to stay for as long as she liked. An absolute train wreck in the making.

"I've made dinner plans with someone."

"The girl I passed on the bridge?" Alicia said.

Even in a smallish cabin, we managed to keep it civil through dinner, but as the evening wore on, Alicia unpacking in her room while Beth and I laughed over photo albums, it devolved into some rather violent drawer slamming. Finally, Alicia threw open her bedroom door and broke out the B-word to describe the reasonable young woman seating across from me. I got out camping gear and asked Beth if she'd like to join me on a backcountry tour of some hot springs I'd discovered.

If Alicia had just gone to bed, Beth and I might not be twenty years down the road together. Go figure. Life is not a box of chocolates, not mine anyway. It's more a funhouse of distorting mirrors and veiled mysteries. Lucky then that Beth found my hand in the dark when she did.

She'd leave a week later, to complete the motion of her national parks greatest hits tour. Gone, but not really. We'd buried the best bits of ourselves together on the other side of a wilderness boundary. Over the next two years, through letters that traveled oceans and continents, we'd get to know each other from the inside out. The right ink on paper can create an out-of-body intimacy. Spirits stripping away everything but their cores. We brought those parts out of hiding through words and doodles, and hiccups of unvarnished truth telling, then held them up to the light when no one was looking. At a certain point, we'd read enough to quit jobs and schools and mix all of it together.

Chapter 17

Crash and Burn

Death is a very dull, dreary affair, and my advice to you is to have nothing whatsoever to do with it.
—W. Somerset Maugham

While working my way to California for the big reunion with Beth, an aging hippie with a hell of a case of acid reflux and a broken marriage took me on an unscheduled detour. It wasn't 9 AM when his Subaru, doing in excess of seventy miles an hour at the time, and in which I was a passenger, achieved liftoff, turning my tunnel of love dark in a hurry.

The last thing I saw as the car used an alligator juniper tree to gain altitude and angle was a postcard I'd been writing to Beth. It floated by as if in zero gravity, then went AWOL between the mountain bikes tumbling around in the cargo space. Tumbling because we'd gone into a midair roll. I grabbed the "Oh Jesus Bar" above the passenger window, but I did not like our chances.

When the showroom-new Subaru first started its drift off the highway I assumed we were pulling over yet again; for endangered roadkill to store as evidence against "the man," for a sacred feather, the usual for Hippie Dan. But no, the tight, straight road to Corona, New Mexico, offered no shoulder and a sixty-degree-angled drop into deep arroyos on either side. Dan was impulsive, unconventional in a haphazard sort of way, but not suicidal.

"Steady," I pleaded with the dashboard. The Subaru, while not gaining speed as it tap-danced along the edge of the cliff, didn't slow down. I caught a glimpse of my driver. Dan's chin was resting peacefully on his chest. Both hands had relinquished their hold on the steering wheel, and his eyes were closed.

Sniper?

Heart attack?

Narcolepsy?

It was too late to stay on the road, but maybe I could control the ride down the steep grade all the way to the softer sand of the dry wash. As a cyclist with some mountain biking credits, I felt like I knew how to manage an off-road experience gone vertical. We needed to angle into it. This might still turn out okay.

I reached for the wheel but reacted too fast. When the seat belt yanked me back and the last of the asphalt ran out I knew with sickening clarity that I was just along for what was left of the ride.

We mowed over a few saplings, no real damage, then the alligator juniper tree jumped into view just above the grille. Stubby and thick, it was probably eighty years old. We hit it head-on. The Subaru took flight, resembling a roller coaster jumping its track at the height of the arc.

The symmetry of dying on one's birthday might smack of goth poetry, but only in the abstract. Yes, it was my birthday. I gripped the bar, attempting to make myself small as the car went into its first rollover, a poor man's space shuttle coming back to earth. The irony was not lost on me that after countless miles of cycling I would die inside a car. The big man likes his comedy black as coal.

On impact, the first of many as the car worked through dozens of rolls, a harsh realization hit. I would be alone at the end. The rag doll in the driver's seat was still out. Someone needed to know how much I wanted to keep the party going. There was plenty of room left in my heart to marvel at the confused spectacle of being alive. Despite jaded moments, I hadn't outlasted my capacity to give a shit.

And I didn't want just any witness, I wanted Beth. Not the dust, rocks, and branches slamming into the shattering glass of the windshield, but Beth. I called out her name. As final acts go, it held dignity. Unfortunately, with the Subaru crushing in around me, my mind filled with another thought, that I let replace Beth's smile and easy laughter in my head.

"Just don't let it hurt . . . Please, don't let it hurt . . ."

When I opened my eyes it took a moment to see if I was still in one piece. Granted, I was upside down in a crumpled vehicle, smoke billowing from the hood and a fence post rammed through the windshield inches from my ear, between myself and Hippie Dan, but I wasn't howling in pain or severed in half, least I didn't think so. I felt around the smoke and dust, fearing that I'd come upon a leg or blood cascading freely from an exposed artery, but all I found was the silence of the desert.

"Okay, no one panic."

Ah, Hippie Dan was back.

Here's what I was thinking. *Enjoy your siesta, brother?*

While you were gone the car achieved a low-altitude orbit and I experienced the most terrifying seconds of my life. And if you hadn't noticed, we're upside down in what's left of a smoldering wreck, so don't tell me what to do.

As I struggled to unclip myself, Dan said something about chilling out. That the worst was over.

I dropped out of my suspension with a dull thud. Upside down in a tight little spot but no longer trapped by the belt. I began kicking the bent metal of the passenger door hard enough to worm through.

"See that smoke, Dano. Do what you want, but she could blow any moment." It looked like I'd made enough space to escape.

"That's only in the movies, man," Dan said, still dangling over the steering column like a fruit bat.

"Where the f-k you think they got the idea?" I yelled over my shoulder, kicking once more before slithering for daylight.

My words must have connected somewhere deeper than the catalog of Phish concerts his mind had on a regular loop, because Dan started moving. I heard a thud drop onto the roof behind me.

Once beyond of the wreckage, I saw that I only had a scrape to the knee. No worse than a child's dust-up with the sidewalk. The car, on the other hand . . . From our vantage point at the top of the arroyo it would be safe to say no survivors. I'd lost count after the seventh or eighth rollover, but that car looked like something put through a rock tumbler.

Most of the windows were shattered; one wheel was completely gone, swallowed up by the desert. The others were folded under the frame at unfamiliar angles. The body was so dented and deformed, I imagined a gigantic hellhound had used it as a chew toy. A thick fence post driven through the front windshield reminded me of a spear that stops a big animal in its tracks.

We waited in silence . . . for the car to blow.

"I'm really not supposed to eat spicy foods." Dan whispered.

An odd bit of trivia to share at a time like this. What was he looking for in return? *That's okay, Dan. Pork medallions in heavy cream sauce give me wicked gas?*

"I'm usually safe unless I drink the coffee too fast," he added.

I looked down at the battered car, then back at him.

"Are you telling me this happened because of breakfast burritos and black coffee?"

Dan studied a cloudless sky.

"It's called a hiatal hernia. Spicy foods make my esophagus close up. I've had my license back for a year now. No incidents."

I took a moment to let it all sink in. This jackass nearly ended my life over his inability to avoid green chiles while operating heavy equipment? I resisted the urge to fling him over the arroyo again, no seat belt this time. But my heart wasn't in it. Despite the laws of physics, and chiles eaten too early in the morning, I'd walked away from another blast zone unscathed.

Birthdays should mean something. This was the first one in some time that felt like a fresh start. I don't put much stock in signs, omens, or magic eight balls (though an eight ball landed me my first kiss, so I have a soft spot for it). But coming out of a battered womb of twisted metal felt like a definite break with the past. There would be no more emotional stuttering when it came to acting on the things I believed. I would sprint into my future rather than sidestep it with detours to tropical islands and adventures across the Outback.

"We can keep the hernia stuff between us, right? If any of this looks like it might start involving the police."

Might start involving the police? Before I started laughing in his face, we spotted a car growing in the distance. I stepped out and waved it down. Hopefully it was the police.

She was an off-duty EMT. An optimist considering she was driving a Miata. She put on the hazards and stepped to the edge of the arroyo.

"My God," she said, reaching into the backseat of her tiny car for a first-aid box. "Poor bastards. You been down there yet to see if anyone's alive?"

Dan reached out to stop her.

"We're the poor bastards," I announced, a bit of pride in my voice, if still some wobble in my knees. "There's no one else down there."

She gave us a look, like maybe we were part of a murder-for-hire operation and we wanted the poor bastards to bleed out proper before anyone got to them.

"He's serious. I was the one driving," said Hippie Dan.

"And I'm the one that was awake," I wanted to add.

She let out a sigh. "Working an ambulance, I see this thing a lot. No one else down there?"

We nodded again.

"Buy a lottery ticket, then. You shouldn't be standing."

That's when it hit me. I shouldn't be standing anywhere but next to Beth. Definitely not in the desert with some astrologically challenged

159

narcissist, his smoldering wreckage, and his trashed marriage.

We leaned against her ridiculously little car. "Let me ask you something. How many smoldering wrecks like that actually blow?"

She smiled. Pointed at the CB on her dash.

"More than you'd think. I've already called the police and fire departments."

Hippie Dan threw his hands up, kicked a few clumps of sagebrush, and huffed around in circles.

Chapter 18

As You Wish

Buttercup: You mock my pain.

Man in Black: Life is pain, Highness. Anyone who says differently is selling something.

—*The Princess Bride*

In less than forty-eight hours I would be in Beth's arms. It felt like a Francis Ford Coppola epic: years in the making, countless miles logged, screen-testing other hopeful leading ladies and sharing time with stand-ins, sleepless nights, and cheating death without the help of special effects, but now it was all behind me, we were going see each other again, for the first time since our walk into the New Mexico wilderness.

When the message that I'd been in a car accident reached her answering machine, Beth didn't wait for a follow-up call, she abandoned her books and final exams for a plane to El Paso, Texas. I got word of her imminent arrival while closing out my last commitment to the federal government. Unfortunately it put me a few miles underground, literally.

My final task involved photographing stalactites and underground rivers with a certain type of lighting equipment that "saw" through the formations. Roger, a hulking geologist who had spent the better part

of twenty years underground on spelunking missions, was the photographer; I was his sidekick. Roger had decent color for a man kept
away from the sun for so long.

"Vitamin D," he explained, handing me increasingly heavier pieces
of camera equipment. I organized these the best I could in my back-
pack. "And mandatory vacation days," he added.

And about his size, I had to ask him how a man shaped like a Dal-
las Cowboy chose tight spaces as a career.

"I think myself small."

I liked his attitude.

We stood in Roger's trailer, which had the appearance of being recently vandalized.

"Here? Just under fifteen years," Roger said.

Clearly, the man lived alone. We stood in respectful silence amid
the squalor for a few moments.

"It's great to have an assistant this time," he said.

Both of us knew he was lying. Capable of hauling his own gear and
then some. We'd be joining a group of students from Prescott College.
They'd been exploring the cave for college credit with Roger for ten
days. Any one of them could have carried his gear, but none had government clearance to—what? Carry government equipment? That I'd
be given such a stamp of approval reflects poorly on our republic. But
there I was, entering a gigantic mouth of rock and batshit on official
government business.

"Ten days they've been rooting around in the dark? How big is this
cave?"

I liked that Roger didn't roll his eyes, snort, or shake his head dis-

162

missively when I asked dumb questions related to his passion, profession, or trailer.

"It's actually a system of caverns and tunnels . . . quite extensive."

That's right, he'd been rooting around in the dark for twenty years.

"Does it hook up with Carlsbad somewhere?"

Roger might have rolled his eyes a little on that one.

I changed categories and asked after the strange combination of water bottles holstered to his belt.

"Why is one of them labeled Nancy, with a laminated picture of the former first lady taped to the side?"

He didn't strike me as a Republican. Anarchist perhaps, Trekkie for sure.

Roger's laugh rattled your thoughts, in a good way. It took you outside your head, where people don't ponder or mull things over.

"Damn, I forgot to get you a pee bottle. Down here we can't leave our waste behind, so you get a ziplock for the solids and pee bottle for the rest. Only you don't want to go mixing up your drinking bottles with other things so that's why my pee bottle has a distinguishing feature."

He held up the bottle to his headlamp. Nancy Reagan's tight smile jutted out. Scary. I took some comfort knowing that by the end of the day she'd be up to her ears in it.

"Decided to name mine after someone I wasn't too fond of," Roger said. "Considering her husband's administration took a big dump on the country, called it progress, then got the middle class to pay top dollar for front-row seats to the poor man's beat-down . . ."

Libertarian?

I eyed his ziplock.

"I take it your bag of solids goes by the name Ronnie then?"

Roger looked at me like I was crazy. "Bags don't get names. We use new ones every time we come down here."

Of course, because that would just be gross. But carrying around the same pee bottle since the last administration was in office . . .

He held up Nancy. "We'll have to share her today, 'cause I'm not going back now for another. But hey, don't treat her like a lady."

The college kids from Prescott were a "can-do" crew considering they'd been roaming in an out of caves chilled to the temp of a wine cellar for nearly two weeks. The strain of being underground for days at a time was showing on some of their faces, but most were still into the formations, the underground lakes, and tight spaces.

Exploring Cottonwood is nothing like strolling through Carlsbad, with its handicapped-accessible gently sloped paths, its ADA-approved rails and lighting, and an elevator at the bottom that jettisons tourists up to the gift shop and café in under three minutes.

Every foot down and every yard back out of Cottonwood Cave, you earned. Spelunking involves ropes and agility and a keen sense of personal space . . . and understanding that the darkness and convoluted shapes of the tunnels are going to violate that space at any moment. You gotta be right with yourself and the universe to muck about down there. Or fake it well. And your movements should be slow and deliberate. Meaning it could end badly for me.

The formations Roger was photographing were needles in haystacks. Ones that would make otherworldly images, but only Gollum or some wonky geologist who had spent years mapping the landscape of these caverns could find them easily.

"This one looks like a dark lord's icy fortress," I mused. "It turns purple when you put light here, but not there. And it's not like the reds and oranges in the last series."

Roger appreciated my enthusiasm. "This place always holds another surprise for me," he whispered. "Just when I think about putting in for a transfer I find a new passage or something like . . . this."

I rotate the light around the stalagmite formation.

"You just found this one?"

His smile was slight but satisfied. "I've seen it a thousand times. But only just now did it show me this hue of purple."

It was very purple.

I wanted to say something like, *The stalagmite formerly known as Prince,* or break into a chorus of "Purple Rain," but for once I located the still part of myself and simply held the light in silence while Roger snapped off a few more images and bowed in the direction of the formation then moved on.

We broke for lunch in a cavern marked by three separate pools of water fed by a subterranean river. Roger told us to turn off all light. I expected total darkness, as I'd experienced at the previous break when he had us power down for no explainable reason. That darkness being so total it made me feel as if I no longer existed. I actually dreaded shutting my light off again, but when you're three miles from the surface you do exactly what the only guy who knows the way out tells you to do. Still, it was my electric torch that went dark last.

This time we weren't left in nothingness but phosphorus lines and fat dots glowing just below the surface of the water. My brain took a few moments to translate what my eyes saw. Everyone gasped; a real Jules Verne moment, bathed in green light. Stunned, humbled, and grateful that I hadn't died in a spicy-food-fueled car crash twenty-four hours before.

No one wanted to turn their light back on. We waited out the last of the glowworms. When they had faded to black, we held off still, comfortable now that something existed in peace in this space outside ourselves, even though we couldn't see it.

When headlamps went back on I realized that I knew everyone's name.

I'd gotten to know them during the four hours of crawling, roping, hoisting, and hiking ever deeper into the planet, trading places along the conga line of headlamps and helmets, chatting with a pair or three of them, before hopscotching to another part of the line: tunnel mingling. In part because I'm a social creature by nature, also so that if I wandered off and got lost I'd have a bunch of names to call out in the darkness.

Mostly, it's that I still liked people, and I still do to this day. Despite everything we do to shake me of this—laying on the horn so they can get to Starbucks twenty seconds faster, Facebooking what they're having for dinner, and complaining about how long it takes to walk around the mall. If this generation were Pilgrims we'd be the ones who died the first winter.

Socializing is also a good way to pick up survival information. Like the alarming fact that while it took us four hours to get down to the glowworm river, it would be another seven before we saw daylight again.

"Remember that vat-like opening we rappelled down this morning?" Wiley, the guy with the track-star body, said. "We're not Spider-Man. At least the rest of you aren't. I'd like to try scaling back up."

And I thought we'd be out by mid-afternoon. Beth had an early-evening arrival time in El Paso. The space closed in even though I still had all three light sources. People were starting to pack up and excuse themselves to spend time with their bottles and bags. That's when I cleared my throat dramatically.

"Roger, is it true we're seven hours from the exit?" I said.

Roger spotlighted me with his headlamp. "Rubbish."

I smiled.

"It can't be more than six, counting pee breaks."

I squatted on a rock formation, using it as a makeshift stage. "I need everyone's attention."

The cave went silent.

"True love," I said.

References from the movie *The Princess Bride* had become catchphrases in pop culture at the time. Some of the Prescott students thought I was clowning at first. They called back, "As you wish, Buttercup," and "Anyone got a Peanut." I soldiered on, weaving a soliloquy in the darkness, squatting there like the frog prince trying to become more.

They realized soon enough that I was serious. Pressed for time, my narrative could only hit the highlights: battles against rednecks, the elements on the day before we'd met, our fateful meeting, the parting, the longing, the reunion, the Alicia episode, my exodus into the wilderness, the letters, the car accident, all culminating in "So you see, my real flesh-and-blood Buttercup can't step off that plane to an empty waiting area. She just can't. True love must arrive in Texas on time. It could, it will, with your help." If I'd had a sword I would have humbly bowed in front of it.

Silence. Either everyone was moved beyond words or just embarrassed for me.

Someone farted, snickering followed. I was done for. Losing the room and I didn't even have that sword to fall on.

"As you wish!" Roger roared. He'd been listening from behind a thick jutting structure. "Just get the hell off my stalagmite. It's unstable to begin with, protected by the government, and you have the grace of a wounded hippo."

Thank God he'd made it out of his cave long enough to catch the most stylish, satirical fairy tale of the decade.

Women, following Roger's cue, cheered. True Love, whether it exists or not, is always a crowd pleaser.

"There is a way," Roger continued. "But everyone has to agree, no wavering, since it's a bit tricky."

The group awaited orders. How tricky?

"I haven't used it since the collapse, but the work crew told me it's passable now, and I can trust most of those guys."

Now the groans. True Love in this corner, personal safety in the other.

"How much time will it cut off the ascent?" asked a shaggy-haired kid. He'd been the loudest groan. You could tell from his glazed-over look and the shuffle in his step he wanted out almost as much as I did. I'd heard him humming snippets from the unexplainably successful

Broadway musical *Cats*. He need out in a bad way. Which could actually work in my favor.

"Forty-five minutes to the cutoff. We'll be outside in an hour and a half," Roger said.

Shaggy Hair brightened.

"But I don't want anyone deciding on the fly," Roger continued. "Go have quiet time with your Nancy bottles or find a spot in the dark to get right with your thoughts. Then we'll take a vote. Everyone's aboard or we don't do it."

Fair is fair. We tackle it musketeer-style or not at all.

My fate rested with a jury of my ecofriendly peers. Tired, at the tail end of their adventure, who among them wouldn't want to chance the shortcut?

It would only take one spelunking addict in the bunch, or an earnest scholar who considered their parents' hard-earned tuition dollars more valuable than some clown's story of true love.

Had I done enough to hammer home themes of lasting affection within a transitory existence? Of seizing the moment, the essence of living fully in time and space and taking the got-damned reigns of one's happiness?

Had I mentioned that I would leave them enough money to get properly soused at the little bar just outside the park service boundary?

From somewhere in the darkness came a voice; my voice as it happened.

"I'll throw in beer money."

A message came down the line. The tunnel tightened ahead, but not to worry, it split in two directions—one funneled down to impossible, the other opened up to where we could crawl again. We'd already been on our hands and knees for fifteen minutes and a small trickle of water had entered the equation. People stopped joking. Only grim determination and the sound of kneepads scraping through the muck filled the narrowing space.

I was second from the end and right behind Shaggy Hair. I thought it best to keep him laughing and distracted since he'd been the last raised hand at vote time.

When conditions forced us to our bellies, all my chatter might have distracted him. Shaggy took a left instead of the instructed right, and within a few yards had managed to turtle himself. Turtling is when the helmet gets wedged into a space that won't easily release it. Since your head is inside that helmet you look like a turtle as you fight against the elastic strap, fleshy face pulling out for an instant before the strap draws it back into the crevice. He was in no danger of suffocating but a nervous breakdown was imminent.

Making matters worse, Shaggy couldn't bring either of his hands around in the tight space without dislocating them. I could see some of this from my vantage point, but there wasn't space enough to reach over and free the helmet. The best I could have managed was to smack his legs like a deranged jockey trying to win the mole rat derby.

As long as Shaggy didn't panic, he would manage to unearth himself.

"Holy shit," I blurted out before I could stop myself. This assessment had him a bit rattled.

"Pull me out," he said in a firm, measured voice, the one people use when they're trying not to lose it. I asked the girl bringing up the rear to wiggle back so I could get some playing room.

"Pull me out." Less measured now. I was still getting into position.

"Now! Pull me out, now!"

Ready or not, I grabbed his ankles. "Dude, maybe try turning your head like a corkscrew as I pull. I'm not gonna yank, just a steady pull."

"Now!" He was mixing hyperventilation with whimpering by then.

Pulling free a fully grown, incoherently blathering man using only your arms while his head is lodged into a murky crevice is a hell of a spot to arrive at in one's life.

True Love takes us to the damnedest places.

First pull . . . nothing. Second go-round I confess to yanking a bit harder. He must have twisted free just before the third pull. His long hair protected much of his face as I dragged it along the cold rock.

"I'm okay. I'm okay. I'm okay," he kept repeating. The girl behind me hollered that she'd found the correct turn and was taking it. We shimmied backward, then worked our way through. After the turtle space it felt like the great outdoors. The rest of the group was waiting for us.

"Everyone in one piece?" Roger asked.

"Barely," I offered, pointing over at Shaggy.

Shaggy cleared his throat. I feared I was in for it.

He pointed his headlamp directly into my face. "True f-ing love, eh? You'd better marry her and cure cancer together . . . or I will hunt your ass down."

Laughter filled the cavern. I was almost out of there and we'd only left bits of skin, most Shaggy's, down there. Nothing could stop me now.

"Well now, you got her stuck good."

He was old but tougher in his eighth or ninth decade than I'd been at my high school prime. Skin of tanned leather, creases resembling trenches across his face. I'd pulled onto what I thought was a feeder road to his farmhouse and now was stuck in the mud. The old rancher patted the hood of my Forest-Service-issue Chevy S-10 and shook his head.

"These things are junk, but that's no reason to ditch it like this." He didn't smile but I thought he might be making a joke.

The tires were mired in muck up to their lugnuts. The last drops of the monsoon drizzled onto his sweat-stained cowboy hat. Lots of people wear the idea of a cowboy hat. He wore the real thing, and without pretense. When he leaned into my passenger window, water dripped off the hat's tip onto the cheap vinyl of the bench seat.

"What made you turn onto this here spit of a cattle path?"

I couldn't meet his eye. "Storm got me turned around, I guess. I was just gonna stop and ask for directions."

"Storm turned you 'round?" He spit into the mud. "Gotta be something more than the storm, if you don't mind me saying, 'cause there's only one road 'tween here and El Paso."

Tell him about true love and how it had me punch-drunk in the heart of the day and twisted up in knots? How it had me thrashing this truck all over the road?

Not a chance.

"You on something?"

I opened the door, stood on the edge of the floor, and waited for him to come up on the other side, then eyed him across the roof. Right in the eyes. We stayed like that for a while.

"No, sir. Just got myself turned around is all. Distracted by some . . . thoughts."

When he smiled, his face deepened, if that was possible. I once watched a bored exchange student make origami shapes out of crinkled paper bags for the better part of an economics class. Fold after fold after fold. It looked like that.

"Well that sounds like the truth. Leave your . . . thoughts and get your stuff and join us for an early supper. This here truck is stuck for the night."

I stood in stunned silence.

"We'll haul the tractor out in the morning and see if it'll catch when the mud's hardened."

He started to move away.

"Hey now." I waved him back. "There's something else." Maybe the timbre of my voice got his attention. Time to find out if that old codger knew anything about true love.

Farmer Horace roared up with the tractor. Either the truck would come free of its muddy trap, or the front end of a government-issue Chevy S-10 would rip clean off in the radiant light of a New Mexico afternoon.

I could have lived happy for the rest of time inside those beats before the moment of truth. This was my last chance to be there when

Beth arrived. I had something outside myself I'd risk it all for. You could go a lifetime and never find that.

Horace was a pro, playing the clutch and commanding the gears of that John Deere like a prodigy. The Chevy caught, slipped, caught again, then inched forward, slipped, rocked, and inched again. When it began to roll back to its resting place once more, Horace sensed the moment from inside his noisy cab. He caught the slack and pulled the rig free in one smooth, triumphant snatch.

I put the puny truck in park, leaned my head against the steering wheel, and allowed myself thoughts of Beth again. In the rearview, I saw Mrs. Horace clasping the old farmer's hand as he walked over to her from the tractor. He tucked her hand in close to his heart, where he'd probably held it a thousand times. True love. Turned out Horace knew a little something about it after all.

And thanks to him I'd have my turn.

PART 4

Prince Rupert to Saskatoon

Mom

*They say you can't take it with you, but I think they're wrong 'cause when
I woke up this morning something big was gone.*
—"Terry's Song," Bruce Springsteen

*Mom didn't learn to drive until she was forty. Being from boarding schools
and after that Manhattan, she never saw the need. Around Pittsburgh we
managed through a combination of walking, buses, and Dad driving us in
his Mustang on the weekends. I loved those walks of my childhood: running
up to the reservoir, walking past the Sears Tower, running sticks along the
wrought-iron fence of the seminary. I knew every yard of our neighborhood
and well beyond.*

*So did my mom. With four children born in six years it was more of
an expedition than a walk each time she left the front door.*

*We tried to keep up the tradition when we moved to Florida, but we'd
moved to a land still being built around us, a place that had forgotten anything existed but the car.*

*Mom passed her driving test . . . eventually. We believe it was a com-
bination of tenacity, patience, and getting an examiner who was either half
asleep on a Saturday morning or still tipsy from the night before.*

*Needless to say, she only drove when there was no other option. My dad
showed us that he knew the score by purchasing the toughest-looking Bon-
neville on the lot. It was even green like a tank. Its bumper was the size of
my first apartment. Which was problematic when Mom turned it against*

her own house. Early one Sunday morning, with Dad shaving in the bathroom before church—he used this as his quiet time and sometimes lost track—Mom decided to get the car out of the garage and warm it up for Pop. That bumper hooked the inside doorway, pulling bricks and part of the electric garage door with it. Mom squealed, panicked, mashed down the gas, and cleared the obstruction with a glorious clamor of mortar, metal, and soft-rock favorites on the stereo.

We said an extra prayer that morning for the structural integrity of the garage, to tide it over until workers could come out to make repairs.

Mom got better behind the wheel but it was never her natural habitat. We'd drive out to the local beach every weekday in the summer, but no matter how many times we covered the same route, Mom was always a virgin. That was the joke among all the kids, and many of our family friends who drove with us on occasion. Years before the invention of GPS I was her in-person OnStar tracking system. We'd pull out of the driveway and I had to call out every left and right there and back no matter where we went. I could carry on full conversations with others while giving directions at just the right time for Mom to have enough distance to react.

I was twelve, not particularly interested in cars, but I could have landed a job with UPS in a heartbeat.

"I feel so much better when you copilot me," Mom said. "How long until you get your license?"

"Years, Mom. Turn left after the International Inn."

On my fifteenth birthday, she handed me the keys with a relieved smile.

"I hope you know where you're going," she joked. "Because I know you're always a virgin behind the wheel."

She'd known about our running gag all along. I think Mom drove bet-

ter than she let on, but it was her way of getting me to come along on things even after I'd grown too old to care about them. Or she didn't, but it still worked in her favor. Thinking back, I wouldn't trade the laughs, the panicked moments of terror when Mom would execute U-turns across three lanes of traffic in the rain, or the time with my younger brothers and sister . . . and with my mom. She was so young and vibrant and always splurged on the newest swimsuits each season. And full of fight against a disease that wanted to put her in a wheelchair, but all the while she wouldn't even let it coax her into driving more than a few miles a week. We still walked around the neighborhood when other families drove by on their way to the corner store . . . with the air-conditioning on and the windows rolled up. We'd wave and keep walking.

These days, when I pick her up at the retirement home, she'll say, "Do you remember the irony of it all? My last job with the school system was to drive *all over Tampa, to the homes of students too sick to come to school."*

I nod.

"I drove every day!"

"And every day, Mom, I lit a candle."

She laughs every time.

"Turn here," she says from the passenger seat, knowing I know the way into my own driveway, but baiting me.

"Thanks, Mom. I'm always a virgin behind the wheel."

She smiles. "What will you do when I'm gone?"

I hold her arthritic little hand in mine.

"Hang up my keys for good, I suppose. And walk, like you taught us."

I come around to her door.

"Shall we?"

Arm in arm we take a stroll down the bluff. I don't know how many more of these we'll get, but we have this one.

As we round the bend, forty years dissolve and for a while I'm a little boy again, on a walk with his mom.

Chapter 19

Selwin Berries

Kindness is the language which the deaf can hear and the blind can see.
—Mark Twain

Lured by the promise of pump-fresh water and primitive camping, we wheeled into a provincial park a day's ride from Prince Rupert. The Prince had become something of a pauper lately. I'd passed through there years before, on my pedaling-and-pool-cues adventure from Chicago to Denali. By all appearances the kingdom appeared to have been ransacked by unemployment and meth since I'd visited.

I talked with a number of locals, and to a man they were trying to claw their way out. I felt like we'd rolled into a Steinbeck novel.[125] The people still there, those were pioneers to say the least. We found the lone bike shop, great folks, but my basement had more inventory. I wanted to but couldn't Slime the rear wheel. Our last stop was a place that sold raingear to fishermen. There I made the smartest purchase of the trip in the form of sealskin sock/booties. I made the worst decision of the trip shopping-wise by not buying Beth a pair.[126] The rest of the gang filled holes in their raingear wardrobes. It's always good to buy what the locals use against the weather.

The sun was out and strong when we shook off the quiet suffering of Prince Rupert. Packed with our last restaurant meal for a while—pancakes and chocolate milk eaten alongside a row of chain-smoking, coffee-drinking lost souls—all we wanted was to feel the miles in our legs again and wide-open space.

Be careful what you wish for.

With no other amenities for a hundred kilometers, the provincial park was getting our business one way or another. Not fifty yards through the entrance, Ranger Selwin blocked our path. My greatest fear was that this grandfatherly-looking type would tell us his campground was full, overrun by bears, closed for repairs, or, most crucial, suffering a tainted water supply.

125. I remember it feeling so far north on the map. It gave me the creeps after the sun went down. We rolled off the ferry once again in the dark. The boys started to whimper out of memories from the ride in and because they were so tired from sleeping in chairs on the boat. When I woke up the next morning I couldn't wait to be rolling again.
126. I was mad when I saw his socks but I probably would have gotten sweaty in them five minutes into each day's ride. Joe was so hot and cold the entire trip he needed them as something of a wet suit for his feet.

What happened next stays with me to this day. In an understated act of goodwill he extended a baseball cap full of thimbleberries.[127]

I started to ask him something, but he waved me off with a smile.

"Eat first, then we'll get to the questions."

We gathered around his outstretched cap. It felt a little like communion, except for the satisfied moaning with each bite of berries.

Before I could get back to my questions, Selwin covered them in a conversational way, even suggesting which site had the best view of the lake, where we could pick more berries, the best path to the swimming hole, and where we could hike to use one of his canoes.[128]

Through a mouthful of fruit Quinn said what we were all thinking: "I like *this* Canada."

127. They weren't thimbleberries. God knows if you ever get Joe as your nature guide. Selwin restored my faith in my fellow man. He also reminded me of all the good times and people we'd already met because of the bike.

128. Sometimes I wonder what people thought of when they saw us coming down the road. Before my transformation I would have thought we were flat-out nuts. Selwin didn't say anything beyond "My . . ." when he took the handlebars of Joe's rig for a minute.

182

The ornate hand pump made you earn every drop of water. The boys turned it into a game, helping other campers fill their jugs and cooking pots until they were breathless and ready for a swim.

"It's freezing!" Enzo said. He'd only made it up to his knees before turning back.

Two little girls were frolicking in the water as though it were Miami Beach. Only they were speaking in another language.

I pointed this out to my boys.

"They must be from Iceland." Quinn said.

Beth, who had been talking to their mom, said, "They're from Finland."

We watched them splash about a while longer.

"Well that explains it," said Quinn, relieved that a pair of little girls had been raised in ice water . . . saving him face and a dip in a cold lake.

Chapter 20

Wilderness Gourmet

May your trails be crooked, winding, lonesome, dangerous, leading to the most amazing view.

—Edward Abbey

The hardest day on any ride never announces itself. You blunder in blissfully unaware and pedal out the other end scorched, shell-shocked, and barely breathing.[129]

Blindsided.

Sure, the Boy Scouts were on to something with the whole "always be prepared" mantra, but it's no fail-safe. The universe has everyone's

129. I can think of at least three different days like this—ironically, not the one Joe's talking about.

number. You may get lost in the backlog for a while, but . . . And don't imagine you can cover all your bets and bases while still walking upright and aware through the world.

When in the thick muck of living, best-laid plans are the first things to go, with rules and restraint not far behind.

Edgy hooligan scouts who find more than merit badges out in the wilderness know this in their bones, by feel or instinct or trial and error—more often than not with two wet sticks during monsoon season. These are the scouts who pick up another affirmation in the face of serious shit-covered fans:

"Endure, brothers, endure."

The look of enlightenment rarely comes without scuffs, bruises, dehydration . . . and the occasional blunt-force trauma.

Maybe some see the face of God by throwing steam on rocks in a little room, holding a lotus position at sunrise, or making four easy payments to the "Unleash Your Core Power" weekend retreat.

For the rest of us, the hard way is all there is.[130]

"It's fresh tar, I think." I stooped over the bike's center bar and touched the blacktop for confirmation. Not my smartest moment. It had the consistency of Laffy Taffy but the sharp edges of broken glass. I pulled my fingers back and swore. Beth shook her head while I used some tall grass to wipe away the blood. The road was smooth and even, but on the shoulders, where one rides a bicycle, this buildup of half-baked highway was conspiring against us. Popping my tires like party bal-

130. And if you're married to Joe sometimes the hard way comes looking for you.

185

loons.[131]

"Everyone off," I hollered. Our third flat tire in an hour. It was threatening to break my good spirits, but the view was to die for and we had spotted our first moose.

Beth came out of her saddle and rounded up the boys for some roadside summer camp. She looked hot. To me she always looks sexy but we're talking twitchy, uncomfortable hot. The gang played Find Some Shade while I rooted around for another tube.

We were out of tubes.

I kept meaning to get the back tire Slimed. Truly. And we weren't out of tubes exactly, we were out of Presta tubes. The rest of the operation runs on Schrader. The back wheel of the tandem is my only Presta holdout. And the only tire in operation that I hadn't had Slimed. It was looking more and more like my Achilles' heel.

131. I wasn't worried about the flats. Joe always got us back on the road, except this time there was less bike clinic and more swearing.

"That's the runner guy," Enzo says. "The one whose mom dipped him in the River Styx . . . but she held the baby by the heel . . . and that's the little piece that didn't get protection."

I stop what I'm doing to give my seven-year-old a fists-together bow from the Karate Kid movies.

That was damn impressive.

When—wait, more importantly, how—did my seven-year-old start channeling a visiting professor of Greek mythology?

Beth anticipated my confusion. "*The Last Olympian* series. Our read-aloud before bed all last spring."

Enzo performed an exaggerated fist bow in my direction. When I returned to the flat tire debacle he'd managed to engage his older brother in a tae kwon do exhibition of kicks and punches among the tall grass. That wouldn't end well, but I was too hot and too focused on finding the source of that recurring flat to give it any energy.[132]

Above them was a road sign I was trying to avoid eye contact with.

TERRACE B.C. 110 KM

Damn, I had to look. Recalling another character in Greek mythology, the fool who gazed over his shoulder at Medusa and her wild head of serpents. Turned to stone right there on the far northern reaches of Canada's highway system. Or my heart's been hardened to asphalt, anyway. The sign confirms that there's no way, not a wing or a prayer we'll make civilization or anything close to it by nightfall. We've already done 70k but it's beyond the center of the afternoon. Terrace might as well be the other side of the moon.

---

132. My strategy is to let them go at it until someone cries three times or there's blood. It sounds cruel but I'd be getting into it all day otherwise.

Which would be fine except we've been handed distressing if conflicting news along the road, fed to us in piecemeal portions. All manner of misinformation and half guesses from highway workers, counter clerks, and gas station attendants. No one can say for sure whether there's anything—food, lodging, even drinking water—between the provincial park we pushed out from at sunrise and Terrace. There's some talk about a beautiful park at the river crossing 60k in. It starts confident but then falters when it's pointed out that said park was shuttered a few summers ago on account of flooding and bugs.

"Water's not a problem anymore, but I know that spot is still out of commission 'cause my sister was its last host. Trust me, she's cooped up with her mom and seven cats too old to clean themselves proper anymore. She'd have been back in a flash if they'd opened it up."

Those must be überbugs then. Canada doesn't close much on account of buggy conditions and wildlife.

Either way we never found the park. If it existed it was miles behind us.

We had supplies, enough water. We could have camped anywhere.

What had me on edge was the sheer size of everything we were cycling through. The valley—formed by glaciers—was so massive I started telling the boys about *Gulliver's Travels,* and by the time we'd played out that theme, I half expected a giant to step over the gap between ridges. In layman's terms I'd freaked myself out a little. The boys were not helping matters by talking now in little high-pitched voices about eagles the size of F-16s swooping down and taking our little pedaling contraption for a flight. I would ask them to stop with the creepy voices, but I started the conversation.

There's an aloneness in spaces this open and untouched that lets a mind wander. Normally, I savored the feeling above almost anything I get to experience in the workaday world. In fact I lived inside this state of mind for several months straight while crossing the Nullabar plains of Australia and credit it for whatever clarity I carried into the next decade of my life.

That day it was eating at me from the inside, swallowing my peace of mind slowly the way a snake takes its time drawing in caught prey.

Exertion, heat, and the beauty of light playing off the canyons squelched the Hills Have Eyes vibe that I'd been cultivating into the late afternoon.

"Psssss . . ."

It was the rear tire on the tandem again, and I was out of tricks or at least tricks that would get us back on the road before nightfall. The last repair involved patches, dollar bills glued on top of those patches, deal making with gods, and a smudging ceremony using the Canadian equivalent of sage.

Emotionally, we were finished, me and that pinch-flatting tube and its conspirator of a tire. I was having trouble even looking at the pair, unless I was swearing into my jersey sleeve or kicking them.

Enzo presented me with a plastic lightsaber. I beat the useless tire a few times, then followed that up with a flurry of swipes and slashes in the general direction of the mountains. There may have been some vocalizing, I don't remember. I nodded over to my son who, with social understanding beyond his years, wordlessly took back the toy and stepped away from my emotional breakdown.

I felt a little better.

At least now I knew the source of my unease. All the weight I was carrying. Not the bike, boys, and diapers but inside my head. I'd made myself responsible for a rolling ship of souls, people who had become the oxygen of my days.

Before entering this cavernous valley we'd been a rollicking carnival on wheels, cirque de cycling, a spectacle of length, girth, and color causing normally restrained Canucks to pull the car over, dig out the camera, and whoop, whoop as we'd coast by. Until today we'd hosted a fairly constant pleasure cruise, led by a devil-may-care captain who, when I wasn't cracking myself up or trying with varied success to amuse my passengers, had everything in hand. Broken chains were opportunities for the family to take a swim break while I'd whip out tools, swirl around the apparatus, even give Quinn, still dripping lake water onto warm asphalt, a *This Old House* how-to tutorial.

All gone now. Replaced by a stowaway traveling under the name of doubt. That shapeless little bastard had me rattled. In cahoots with the growing shadows, the broken bike, and all the misplaced confidence pouring out from behind the eyes of my crew.

Decisive action was called for. I visualized Popeye cracking open a can of his best green stuff, but that only succeeded in making me hungry.

We shifted all weight off the rear wheel of the tandem. I instructed Quinn to balance on the front tip of his seat and think light.

"I have a plan," I said.

Beth smiled from her spot perched on a fully functioning bike. Doubt couldn't hope to penetrate her newly buffed arms. Despite the heat, the extra miles, and the time of day, Beth was on summer break from teaching hardscrabble inner-city high school students. Surrounded by majestic solitude and her family—she was untouchable. She'd earned this joy and was taking it.

I tried to tap into that good cheer before setting the bike train into motion—a slow unsteady crawl through the valley. We were on a bit of a slope so it was about keeping the bike under control as we coasted along. Adding another level of difficulty, we'd blown out the backup disk brake during one of the earlier flats. Because it was used only on the steeper grades to slow our rig through flutter actions and coordinated finessing, I'd deemed it a time-wasting repair, better tackled at the camp stop. With the rear rim rolling with little more than compressed rubber between it and the pavement, I didn't want to apply the hand brake too hard. We were going even slower than I imagined because of it.

The only reason we hadn't thrown in the towel and set up camp had to do with our last human encounter, maybe twenty miles back.

Rocking chairs of every stripe loaded down the back of a maroon El Camino. Different eras, woods, makes, models, and degrees of craftsmanship.

The driver, a bearded grandfather type but sturdy and clear-eyed, had set up one of his rockers in front of the Camino's grille. We nearly missed him, but for one sharp whistle he cut loose with as we passed. I circled back, fearing no traffic since his was the first car we'd seen, parked or otherwise, in hours.

Leashed to the arm of the rocker was a dog, the most inappropriate dog for that setting I could imagine. In our house we call them wiener dogs. If it broke free of its leash I'd put its survival among the numbers of eagles, falcons, and hawks we'd seen in trees, in cliff nests, and on the wing at about thirty seconds.

"That's quite a setup," he said.

I was thinking the same thing of his stacks of chairs roped and secured in a manner that would have delighted the surreal artist Escher.

Even at one year old, Matteo went crazy for dogs. Later to be replaced by trains, especially ones named Thomas, but the wiener dog and my third son began bonding immediately in some shared language of chirps, barks, and laughter.

"You make rocking chairs?" I asked.

"Yes." A long pause. "But not these."

We waited, but no further explanation was forthcoming. Instead, he wanted to hear about the best parts of our adventure, which is like asking us to deposit the contents of an ocean we've been swallowing by the mile from our puffed cheeks.

We popped off a few episodes, but it's more light than heat, offering a sense of our epic without much substance. He seemed into it, though, rocking up a storm while quieting his dog with a quick snatch of the leash.

Quinn wouldn't let the mountain of rocking chairs lie.

"Do you sell them in a store?"

That made him chuckle. No store. No.

"The saddest damn thing in the world is a rocking chair in a window where no one can sit in it."

A crazy thought crossed my overheated brain. Maybe we've come face-to-face with Canada's Robin Hood of rocking chairs. He roams the land, looking for underappreciated and unrocked chairs trapped inside rich estates, retail outlets, and old barns. He brings them to people who pledge to rock the shit out of them, evangelical rockers willing to put in the porch time, creaking and gliding and watching the world go by. Sign me up.

I was only half wrong.

"What I do, I buy, beg, scavenge, and ask around for donations of old rockers. I'm retired, you see, so I have the time and the workshop to get 'em back into shape. Anymore, people bring the chairs to me."

Enzo pointed at the El Camino mountain. It looked like the Grinch's toy-loaded sleigh as he balanced it between heartbreak and Christmas morning. For my money, those were the best eyebrows in all of animation.

"Are you coming or going with these chairs?" my son asked.

The guy stopped rocking. "These, eh? They're ready to go. I've repaired all of them, including the one I'm sitting in here. You wanna give it a spin?"

Quinn looked quite comfortable rocking in the shade of a big tree.

The old man was awash in accomplishment. Placid and humble. A quiet realization of one's usefulness in an increasing disposable world.

"Where do you take them now?" I asked.

"I'll tell you, but you being a writer, I don't want this out there in the *Sunday Mail,* looking as if I'm tooting horns or seeking publicity."

We waited. For years I worked as a journalist for a daily newspaper. Promise nothing. Smile, but never, ever, under no circumstances, kill a story before you know how it ends.

"I give 'em away, eh?"

See? That's a scoop. Little light on details, though.

"Do you have criteria for who gets one?"

"Nope."

I opened my mouth but the next question wasn't there. Nope? Nope? That just didn't make sense.

He must have sensed my confusion.

"Well, that's not really true. What I mean is I don't deliver them all to retirement homes or churches or a school library . . . I've given plenty away to all of those places, but the way it works, see, I take a road trip like I'm on right now. I poke my head in everywhere and I ask people where they'd set up a rocking chair if they had one. Depending on their answers I either keep on down the road or ask 'em if they'd like to pick one out. Sometimes I'll set up in a park or front of a library. If you ask for one outright, like you've heard I'm giving away free chairs, I don't give one to you, but if you tell me of someone you think could use one, I make an effort to track those people down."

It was already a long, hot frustrating day, and we were making it longer by visiting with the rocking chair crusader. We'd been chatting awhile, long enough to let Beth catch up to our mule train . . . but sometimes I have to fight the urge for movement, after all, this is why we took to the road by bike in the first place.

This, right here, rocking chair man, *was* the ride.

While telling his story he'd brought down three more chairs and placed them around as casual as if we were in his living room. I couldn't resist sitting in the afternoon sun a bit longer, gently rocking a few yards off the highway. Except for the fact that we were in the great outdoors, a well-crafted rocking chair really ties a room together. It felt as if we'd carved out a sacred little spot of indoors, an inviting sanctuary just waiting for a fireside chat.

Beth is one unflappable individual. I know it takes a true pioneer to manage a daily regime with me, but it did not go unnoticed the way she eased the bike to the ground, pulled food stocks from the front bag in one fluid motion, slipped baby Matteo off the rocker into her arms, and began rocking herself in what I learned was a Mennonite-crafted dark wood model. No fanfare, no double takes or finger pointing over to El Camino mountain or the cracker barrel session that had materialized in the middle of the road to nowhere.

Bend with the road or it will chase you home.

"Any other rules to giving away these chairs," I said, admiring the smooth, worn finish of the one I was rocking in.

He accepted a handful of Beth's gorp with a nod.

"I don't pick out the chairs for them. They find the one that feels right, looks right, that speaks to them, or I tell them to be patient, I'll look 'em up the next time through. I can see it in their face and their body language. If the chair isn't for them I know."

We learned that his handiwork populated not only porches and the entrances to general stores, but fire stations, prisons, bookstores, and bars.

I leaned back in my rocker. I could have slept right there, but something pulled me into the moment.

"Hey, we keep hearing rumors about a beautiful lodge in the middle of nowhere about forty kilometers up the road. Gourmet food, rooms, and campsites. Other people tell us it went out of business, or closed for renovations this summer, or it never existed except in people's imaginations."

The sturdy old man drummed the arm of his rocker, tossed back a handful of almonds and raisins before smiling.

"Oh, it exists. And when you get there, try out their rocking chairs," he said. "Some of my best work."

I hammered him for specific directions but the best I could get was that if I crossed the second overpass after the river we'd gone too far.

His final instructions didn't leave me flush with confidence.

"I don't know if there's a sign. It sits off the highway a couple hundred yards on the left so you could miss it. It has a circular driveway, giving you two chances—should be fine. If you pass it, though, there's nothing else between here and Terrace, eh?"

"Not even a rocking chair?" I joked.

He put the wiener dog into the front seat.

"Not one of mine."

Limping forward on rims, good intentions, and suspect directions—I continued to hold out hope.

But doubt was still on my shoulder and fear was climbing up to join him. I didn't want to plant my family out in the open of this valley if there was a wilderness Shangri-la a few kilometers down the road. If only I could rocket forward to see if the lodge really existed. According to all the tea leaves and mile markers we had to be close.

"Baby needs to nurse," Beth announced.

I'd been ignoring the baby's needs for a few miles. Now I felt like a bad parent on top of a lousy leader.

That's when it hit me. While she was busy, I'd strip Beth's bike to the bone, carry a bit of water and a tool kit, and cover the kilometers to the lodge in minutes, confirming its existence and getting back before they missed me.

I shared my plan while stripping the bike and strapping Beth's panniers onto the sides of the trailer.

She put up no resistance.

"Whatever. We'll keep walking the mule train in that direction. There's only the one road. Just don't do anything stupid like keep looking for it all the way to Terrace."

I was on fire with this idea. The equivalent of bring down the mammoth for my little tribe. I felt proactive and energized.

And going from the five-hundred-pound mule train to an unloaded performance bicycle was like strapping a rocket to my seat. If bikes had headrests I'd have been pressed against it by my first dozen pedal strokes.

Adding to my speed out of the blocks, the downward slope and a solid tailwind made my family dots on the landscape in no time. I was giddy with my progress and the very bearable lightness of being. I stood and hammered the pedals, reaching speeds I'm rarely comfortable with . . . except then. I felt born to go at that speed . . . forever. Doubt and fear dropped their grip as I went into a curve. A revival was taking place in my legs and it was working its way north.

Once clear of the slalom course of curves and tucked into another straightaway, it dawned on me. I was out of sight of my family in an entirely separate, smaller valley and putting more distance between us with every stroke. A cardinal rule had been broken, a line had been crossed—separating from the group voluntarily and for no good reason is the point in the made-for-TV movies where everything goes horribly wrong. And what a place to go rogue, in one of the last North

American strongholds where large predatory animals roamed free and in numbers.

You could smell rubber burning at how hard I braked. In the silence of those long summer shadows falling across the canyon, I shivered at what I'd done. We made our stands as a family, damn it. I vowed to keep them safe but I couldn't fight off a griz or keep a mountain lion from dragging one of my boys into the bush if I was miles away.

Pedal together or die alone.

This was my chant on the long harsh ride back up the incline and into a killer headwind. I deserved it for abandoning my station, leaving a listing ship of trusting souls because I needed speed, closure, and action.

I worked so hard that I ran out of water, but doubled my efforts in spite of burning quads and chalky lips, sure that a marauding pack of animals had them surrounded or a carload of psychopaths was at that moment talking my precious, perfect family into a ride.

When something resembling a caravan came into view—moving along the side of the road in the distance—I went into a flat-out sprint. This could be a cruel but effective training model for elite racers: Tell them their family is in jeopardy and watch records fall.

I came in hot and fast. My family appeared unharmed, happy even, as they walked along. Beth guided the massive bike train down the slight slope with Quinn and Enzo holding the back of the trailer as they talked, in no particular hurry. Panting, covered in sweat, more than a bit of a wide-eyed madman, I dumped the bike and ran across the road.

"Is something chasing you?" Quinn asked.

I went right for Beth, pulled her close in my best Jimmy Stewart from the final scene of *It's a Wonderful Life*.

"Boys, boys . . . leave that and get over here."

I put my foot on Matteo's trailer so that now I had everyone who mattered to me connected in a circle of love.

"Let go of us, smelly man," Beth said, squirming away. There was no malice in her voice, just physical revulsion. The boys laughed as they broke free.

"It's like you took a shower in your clothes," Enzo noted.

"I never should have left you guys," I said. "I got down the road into the next valley and I felt it aching in my bones. The worst decision I've ever made."

"Was it a bear, Dad?" Enzo offered, shrugging as if to say, *It's okay if you were scared*. I shook my head. My heart so swollen with feeling for them. Since hugging was off the table, I tussled Quinn's hair and blew Beth a kiss. She nodded.

"Listen to me, troops."

When I call them troops they flinch. It means a speech is in the making.

"You've been gone all of fifteen minutes," Beth said, hoping to nip any heartfelt band-of-brothers soliloquy in the bud. We were still in the middle of nowhere, burning daylight.

I looked each of them in the eyes, trying to transfer the depth of emotion, but I felt the moment slipping away.

"Pedal together or die alone," I opened with. It was more platitude than rallying cry.

"Pedal together . . ." I trailed off.

Beth's face lit up. Finally, I was making some headway. She felt it. She knew I'd always be there for them, leading our family into whatever came next.

Beth started laughing.

"What?"

"It's taken half of Canada, but you've just figured out how much you need us, is all."

That forced me to take a minute.

How does that woman always have my number?

That was it. For years I'd adventured solo, taking responsibility for myself and the consequences. And when I pulled the boys across America it was never in doubt who was in charge. Had something happened I would have accepted blame. But crossing Canada with Beth was forcing me to let go.

No easy trick for a control freak.

Someday I'd return to the saddle solo to cover big chunks of the planet, but I couldn't imagine rolling anywhere now without, as Zorba the Greek put it, "Wife, kids, the whole catastrophe."

Equal shares and stakes.

"Did you find the lodge, Dad?"

I shook my head. Quinn shook his back. The old man could be a thorough disappointment sometimes.

"But it's fine with me if we want to set up along this road somewhere. We have everything we need right here."

And we did; food, water, shelter, one another.

Beth wasn't having any of it. She handed me the handlebars of my mule train. Her expression said, *Don't go all sentimental. Bring excitable*

Joe back for a bit.

"I'd like a wilderness lodge with gourmet food and a nice rocking chair, if that's all right with you."

She retrieved her own rig and took the pole position.

Two of my three sons spell well enough to know there's no *i* in *team*. Today their old man taught them there's no alternative spelling that includes "jackass thinking he's got to carry the weight of the world and every decision from Portland to Halifax" in there, either.

Beth was done waiting.

"I know it's like riding through our own Ansel Adams photograph," she said, "But let's only camp in this pebbly waste if we don't find the lodge before nightfall."

Still wobbly and surely doing damage to the tire, if not the rim, I pedaled over ground I'd already covered, only this time I knew where I was in the batting order. Comfortable, at last, with someone else leading the charge.

It felt . . . surprisingly good.

The Wilderness Lodge boasted not only signs announcing its presence, but flags flapping in the evening breeze. Or they would have been flapping if there was any blowing. Between the heat and mosquitoes, there wasn't any room left in the world for a breeze.

Even on rims, I overtook Beth for the final stretch into the lodge side road. It wasn't ego this time but elation. We were over the hundred-mile mark for the day and I felt each one of them, not counting my come-from-behind imitation of Greg Lemond's final charge in the 1985 Tour I'd performed on Beth's bike a few miles back.

I looked over my shoulder for good measure, making sure Beth was still in sight.

When the lodge came into view, it was a storybook ending. I'm grateful beyond words that someone's foolish dream of starting a business in the middle of nowhere remained a reality.

There were signs of life right off the bat: an air conditioner purring from a side window, vehicles in the gravel lot, and rocking chairs on the side porch.

That furniture-restoring SOB wasn't delusional after all. Or a heat-stoked mirage of our making.

Kelly stepped onto the landing. He couldn't have been more than a few years out of college, drying his hands the way one does coming from a kitchen.

He waved as though expecting us. We exchanged pleasantries, hitting it right off with his comment, "That's what you call an SUB, eh?"

Quinn liked that so much he'd use it in future conversations.

Kelly said that since we were his only customers, we could have our pick of any room.

"Do you have campsites?" I asked, Beth rolling to a stop by my side.

Kelly looked from me to my lovely bride, who was distracted by a cloud of mosquitoes the size of big toes. She was swatting at the air and performing a duck-and-weave move that recalled a young Muhammad Ali.

It was true that we hadn't had a proper bed in more than a week. The closest was when we contoured ourselves into sloped positions across seats aboard the Inner Passage ferry.

Beth dropped her bike and made for the front door without another word.

"I guess we'll see those rooms," I said.[133]

It wasn't on the menu, but Kelly poured fresh-brewed tea over ice, added milk, and kept me in my favorite drink the rest of the evening. Beth tried to order one half of the menu, I wanted the other, but our host told us to put those things down, he was a culinary-institute-trained chef and if we'd allow him to take care of us, we wouldn't regret it.

The boys were elbow-deep in a pasta-and-cheese combo that to call mac-and-cheese would be like kicking sand in Kelly's eyes. To this day my sons' shoulders sag a little when facing down a plate of standard noodles.

Between our third and fourth courses of ambrosia heaped on big plates, Beth high-fived me.

"We limped in on rims, and look at us now."

I've known Beth nearly half her life and not once had she initiated a high-five, and only begrudgingly responded to my raised hands in her face.

She was still wearing her bike gloves, and did I hear her say that we "limped in on rims"? I'd marry this woman all over again.

We were given a choice between homemade apple and blueberry pies or cheesecake—so we had them all.

By then Kelly was like family, hooting from the kitchen at some of

133. You couldn't have gotten me to set up my tent at gunpoint.

our stories and telling us a few of his favorite moments from working a summer at the lodge. He let us use the Internet and not only offered a complete workshop for bike repairs, but accompanied me so we could drill out the rim to fit my Presta tubes in that troublemaking rear tire. Remarkably, the rim was okay, but we smoothed it down with a metal sander just to be on the safe side. I slept easy knowing the mule train shouldn't give me any problems for a thousand miles . . . and it didn't after that.

When we came back in the boys were mistreating a big bearskin rug in the great room of the lodge. Quinn was wearing it like a cape while Enzo whacked at him with a lightsaber.

I began the "respecting others' property" speech but was cut off when Kelly emerged from a side room with a second bearskin rug draped over his shoulders.

Mayhem ensued. I asked if there was a third rug anywhere.[134]

We were having a nightcap. Beth and the boys, after proper showers, were tucked under clean sheets in the recesses of the lodge.

Kelly mentioned that it was his last week at the lodge. It would be shutting down for the season, and he wouldn't be back next summer.

"I'm helping a friend open a restaurant in Edmonton. He's really good. Trained and worked down in San Francisco for years."

Having lived in the Bay Area off and on, I asked where he'd worked.

"All over, but the one that might mean something to you is this place called The Trident. Famous, on the water. This rock promoter named Werber who knew everyone. Robin Williams bused tables there."

"Frank Werber?"

Kelly looked at me. "You heard of him?"

Heard of him? I knew the man quite well. If it was the same guy, and it had to be. Frank saved my ass when I was managing an arts council in Silver City. But not before he hung me out there. See, we'd booked a group he once managed, the Kingston Trio, for two nights of performances and a big dinner and autograph signing. Word got back to the band through someone, probably Frank, that we were selling tickets to the dinner and autograph-signing session. The boys were not going to show for the dinner and I wouldn't have known about any of it, except that Frank tipped me off. I asked him what could be done, and even though he was well into his sixties, he put on his *I'm still a*

134. I see a grown man in a bear rug, I know Joe has something to do with it. Sometimes I yell at the kids to knock some racket off and it's Joe doing it.

player hat and said he'd see what he could do.

The Kingston Trio came to the dinner, signed everything, and said they appreciated that all the money was going to support local arts projects. I never found out if Frank was full of crap on that one but he did come to the dinner with the trio by his side. So I think he was actually looking out for my interests. Either way, it's how we became friends.

"Stan knew Frank, too. It really touched him when Frank died."

"Frank's dead?" I slouched in the chair. When people overuse the phrase *larger-than-life character,* they need to check themselves with the legacy of Frank Werber. His obit in the *Chronicle* for better and worse, brings this into focus:

> If anyone ever lived up to the image of the swinging 1960s hipster, Frank Nicholas Werber was the man.
>
> The original manager of the Kingston Trio and a successful restaurant and business owner, he had been living it up for several years by the time the Summer of Love rolled around. The bearded entrepreneur wore beads and a tweed coat with a flower in the lapel. There were sports cars, miniskirted young ladies, a penthouse office in San Francisco, sailboat cruises in Mexico, and pot. Lots of pot.
>
> Narcotics agents said six sea bags full of marijuana were delivered to his swanky home overlooking Richardson Bay in 1968, leading to his arrest, two sensational trials and a six-month jail sentence in Marin County.
>
> The charismatic hippy music agent died May 19 of heart failure in Silver City, N.M., where he had lived on a ranch since 1974.
>
> Born in Cologne, Germany, in 1929, Mr. Werber spent time in a Nazi concentration camp during the Holocaust.
>
> He told his family that he and his father were at one point lined up to be shot by a Nazi firing squad when an officer ordered the elder Werber pulled from the line. As the story goes, the officer didn't want to lose the camp's best cook. Because his father wouldn't leave without him, Mr. Werber, too, was saved. The father and son later escaped, although details about that are vague.
>
> Mr. Werber learned to cook from his dad, and from then on, good food played a major role in his life.
>
> He immigrated to the United States. After high school, he joined the Navy and served as an aviation photographer, midshipman and sharpshooter. He later attended the American Academy of Art in Chicago and the University of Colorado.

Family members said Mr. Werber worked as a commercial artist, gold miner, cabdriver, horse rancher, ski-lift operator, construction worker and press photographer.

He eventually landed in San Francisco, where he met Enrico Banducci, the renowned North Beach impresario who operated the hungry i nightclub. Mr. Werber impressed Banducci and was hired as manager.

He stayed at the nightclub for four years and then happened upon a group of young Stanford singers at a bar and signed them to a management contract. The Kingston Trio soon blossomed into a national sensation, ushering in a folk music movement that lasted through the 1960s.

Mr. Werber turned out to be a masterful promoter. He created a multimillion-dollar recording studio and promotional development and publishing company called Kingston Trio Inc., which took up two floors in the Columbus Tower office building.

He then established Sausalito's famous Trident Restaurant, which started out as a jazz hot spot in the 1960s. Mr. Werber later turned it into a psychedelic health food restaurant with hanging plants and handmade candles where rock musicians hung out and ogled braless waitresses.

The now-defunct restaurant, on Bridgeway, set aside a table for Janis Joplin, and a young Robin Williams worked there as a busboy, according to Mr. Werber's daughter, Chala Werber.

"Everyone who was anyone hung out at the Trident," she said. "He interviewed all the waitresses, and they had to be super hot. They weren't expected to wear a bra."

When Native Americans occupied Alcatraz from 1969 to 1971, the pier outside the Trident was used to ferry supplies to island dwellers. In 1974, the Rolling Stones held a private party at the Trident thrown by Mr. Werber's good friend Bill Graham. It was, according to several revelers, a mind-altering experience.

Erudite and witty, Mr. Werber had a financial interest in the hit show 'You're a Good Man, Charlie Brown." He was active in numerous sports, including sailing and scuba diving, which he practiced often in the tropical waters off Puerto Vallarta.

He was, by all accounts, on top of the world in 1968 when federal agents raided his Marin County home and seized 258 pounds of Mexican pot they accused him of conspiring to transport.

Mr. Werber admitted smoking pot, but said he never trafficked in it. He argued that he was set up by dealers who were trying to save their own skin. A federal court jury eventually found him not guilty after a widely publicized trial. He was then tried by Marin County authorities for possession and cultivation of marijuana.

Mr. Werber was defended by Terence Hallinan, who would later become San Francisco's district attorney. The trial was a circus. Sheriff's officers dragged sea bags full of pot into the courtroom, and Hallinan talked about Mr. Werber's spiritual connection to pot rooted in his experiences during the Holocaust. Celebrities marched in and out of the courtroom as a fan club of young women in miniskirts rooted for Mr. Werber, who, participants said, smoked pot a few times during the breaks.

Mr. Werber loved to recount how Tommy Smothers of the Smothers Brothers testified that he had known the defendant for years and "before he started smoking pot, he was a real a-hole."

"It was a pretty interesting trial," said Smothers, 70, a longtime friend who got a big laugh when he testified. "It was very stressful for him at the time, but he just moved on."

Mr. Werber retired at age 43 to an old adobe lodge on 160 acres of wilderness in New Mexico once used by Teddy Roosevelt on his hunting expeditions.

"Everything my dad ever did, he did completely," his daughter said. "His philosophy was there is nothing worth doing that isn't worth overdoing. There was never any half-assing in anything in his life."

Smothers said: "He was a little slick, a little slippery and wonderfully funny and entertaining. He was a guy you would go out of your way to visit."

Besides his daughter Chala, he is survived by another daughter, Mishka Werber, sons Bodhi Werber and Aari Werber, stepson Daniel Benavidez and two granddaughters, all of Silver City.

Kelly and I talked about lots of things that evening, but rest assured, nothing topped the news that Frank Werber had shaken off his mortal coil. The afterlife just got rowdier. We toasted a man Kelly never knew, but wished he had, and I, on occasion, knew too well.

In the morning two gents bike touring from Prudhoe, Alaska, to South America rolled in for breakfast. Kelly heaped their plates as if he was trying to clear out the freezers before the lunch rush.

"Do you get a lunch rush?" I asked.

He looked at the ceiling, thinking hard. "Once. A tour bus showed up, I suspect broken GPS or poor sense of direction. So many folks crowding the place, I fed some of them out on the porch."

"Why are you biking in flip-flops?" Quinn asked one of the cyclists. Since I won't allow my sons to pedal in open-toed shoes, I knew the source of Quinn's questioning.

You could tell that the guy in the flip-flops was happy someone asked.

"Early this morning I heard rustling outside the tent. Through the slit near the window I saw a pair of fox, is it fox or foxes, plural? Anyway, I watched them stealing my bike shoes left just outside the entrance but it didn't register that it was really happening until they were trotting away."

The other guy leaned across the table, grabbed some ketchup for his hash browns, then added, "My fault, I make him leave 'em out there on account of the smell."

And who among us has not asked a friend or loved one to put those stinky things the hell outside.

"Did you follow the foxes?" Enzo inquired.

"Yep, and they led us on a bit of a chase . . . that ended down at the river, where a family of bears were waiting."

There was a silence as all of us adventure seekers on bicycles who sleep out in the woods pondered this.

Quinn nodded over to his brother. "Shoes inside the tent from now on."[135]

---

135. These guys were really nice. We rode with them for a chunk of that day. Joe gave Flip-Flop a pair of river shoes. And they even pedaled in the back with me for a while; Joe's always a few hundred yards to half a mile ahead of me. But what I remember most about them was when Joe gave them the shoes and we offered some snacks from our supplies, standard practice among touring cyclists. They returned the favor with the most unappealing items—I remember them offering me powdered milk, maybe because I was a nursing mother? And crushed, no-name protein bars of the worst flavors. I mean, if we were in an Andes plane crash I might have brought myself to sample the turd-shaped bars over say, human flesh, but only a few short hours after Kelly's wilderness gourmet breakfast? Please. To recap, flip-flop guys great, but if you run into them, bring your own food . . . and maybe an extra pair of shoes.

Chapter 21

Wendy and Her Lost Boys

Forget them, Wendy. Forget them all. Come with me where you'll never, never have to worry about grown-up things again.

—Peter Pan

Restocked, repaired, and rejuvenated by our stay on Ferry Island, we set out late in the morning, bathed in full sunlight, packing vigor, and reeking of hope. Little did we know that this light and heat would be summer's parting wave. Hills and headwinds tried to break our good

cheer in short order, but we'd crossed the line. Once a garden-variety bike touring family, now we were battle-tested travelers.[136]

"So this is a headwind, huh?" Beth asked. It was a rhetorical question, so I kept drinking my Powerade and tried to find a gear that would allow me to stop weaving the mule train all over the shoulder of the road.

I wanted to tell her it was more than a headwind. The wind carried much more today. Something instantly familiar—for the way it showed up on the angle of the sun to the horizon and the slightest shift in everything . . . from the pitch of the cicadas to the way the grass felt when we stopped for lunch in an open pasture.

---

136. Joe felt the temps more I think because he was covered in sweat 24/7. To me it was fantastic to feel a bit of a nip in the air.

Autumn had arrived when I had my head down, grinding out hard miles. I wasn't ready for my favorite time of year. Not yet, but as soon as I felt it on my face I remembered why I love it. Rage, rage against the dying light and all that. I'm Irish. Finding the beauty in decay is my birthright, but beyond all the death poetry written in its honor, for my money it's as much about possibilities, what can still be done in the time that remains. If winter were to knock my crisp new season right off the calendar—a distinct possibility this far north of the equator— I'd have to file a complaint. We had a lot more of Canada to cover and while I would embrace the shortening days and a slight nip in the air . . . Flurries and real windchill? This would not do. We needed a mellow patch of Indian summer until we could get farther south, hug the border somewhere around the center of the continent, and grab hold of the eastern seaboard's lingering color and warmth.

More immediately, Cedarvale was our destination, almost due north of Ferry Island, thirty miles shy of Alaska. Yikes. A bolt of excitement coursed through my muddy heart at the sight of a road sign for the Alaskan Highway. Stewart was just a short ride from there, but any side trip to say we stepped on American soil would have to wait.[137]

The country we were riding through was as stunning as it was brutal on bike riders. Hills appeared as far as the horizon. Not one dramatic climb, but a rolling landscape that means one thing to a cyclist: Prepare to feel the burn. The burn of all-day rollers speaks two languages: hope and ruin. The climbs and downhill tucks are short enough to tempt

---

137. Just after that sign, we saw locals standing on rocks far down below the bridge spear fishing for salmon. It wasn't hard to imagine the same image two hundred years ago.

you to stand up and hammer in the big rings—repeatedly unleashing muscles not accustomed to servicing you more than a few times a day. When you press them again and again they oblige, but damn if they don't hold a grudge. Payback is hell.

For the downhill runs, you pop your keister up and lean deep and heavy over the handlebars. By day's end your arms feel like rubber and your buns of steel are shaking like an old dog's hind legs. But the pain and suffering come later; after sticking the dismount and bedding down for the night, you'll be in ruins.

Hope and ruin. Rollers, the bilingual course you won't realize you signed up for until it's too late.

Seeing as there's one route east, we had no say in the matter. At least we'd turned away from the wind and were making the most of momentum into each roller, counting ourselves lucky that autumn was keeping temperatures bearable for our labors.

Cooler temps are doubled-edged swords for a man hauling a prairie schooner on bike wheels. The rest of the family was working hard, but I consistently achieved a waking dream state reached only by Sufis through days of unbroken whirling dervish dancing. It was rare when my heart rate dropped below 180. The sweat soaking into my jersey was prolific. Which was why cooler temps worked against me. While riding I was golden, but when we stopped, since I was wet from head to heels, I cooled down in a hurry—right past comfortable and into teeth-chattering territory if I wasn't standing in direct sunlight, or when a breeze kicked up. On longer stops, I made quick outfit changes, did jumping jacks, or stripped down to just my bike pants because it was warmer than standing around with a soaked jersey clinging to my chest.

Imagine driving by on your retiree tour of Canada's national parks to catch sight of a shirtless man in tights leading a gaggle of blond boys in a round of jumping jacks, a hoagie sandwich sticking half out of his mouth the way a pelican holds a fish.

"Look, honey, the Boys from Brazil have restarted some bizarre training facility out in here the middle of Canada. I knew this place was a hotbed for terrorism."

It's no surprise there was a lot of picture taking by nameless bystanders and passengers hanging out car windows.

Even though I knew my body would pay later for the repeated camel humps of highway, I savored the ups and downs, the rolling of metal and rubber with my family on the first day of the harvest season.

We found ourselves in this untethered state of grace while so many decent people were caught inside suits, cell phone conversations, and cubicles, making the world run busy and beyond capacity.

Wondering, during brief lulls, just what the hell they were doing it all for.

No one has yet outrun the big, dark machinery that's been set in motion by wishing for too many things we don't need, not for long anyway, but that afternoon in northern Canada, seven wheels and five vital signs cleared the perimeter, and with any luck we'd manage to stay missing for a while.

A few miles short of Cedarvale a cold mist of rain began to fall. We still had our game faces on. The boys zipped on rain jackets and we agreed, even though we'd pedaled through lunch, to turn off the highway and see if we could poke our heads into the Cedarvale First Nation museum. This town had its name on maps, so surely we'd find food, if not on the same street as the museum, then close by.

Anytime we passed a highway sign announcing the border of another community, we'd sound off a few celebratory hoots and yelps.

The main highway continued up, the turnoff headed down.

I couldn't help but smile. We were choosing the path of least resistance for once.

The turnoff devolved from asphalt, to gravel, to mud in less than a mile. I was forced off the rig, pushing the bike up a steep grade of muddy track, cursing myself for diverting from the plan.

All to see some local art.

Beth recognized my mood swing for what it was, low blood sugar. I accepted her granola bars and a hard-boiled egg she'd been hiding in her back jersey pocket. We found the museum at the bottom of the hill. Caked in mud by then, we shot each other confused looks. Where was the rest of the town? The museum consisted of little more than a run-down cottage in the woods and rusting lawn furniture—and it was the most substantial architecture around. The double-wide trailer going back to earth in the adjacent lot was a distant second. A sign hammered into the mud told us we were standing on the future home of the new museum.

Unless we had a time machine we were out of luck.

No one bitched. It was part of the drill. Sometimes you're the bear, sometimes you're chased by one.

I pedaled and pushed our mule train for the better part of half an hour before we met back up with the Yellowhead Highway. As we reached it the rain stopped. I nearly wept with relief. A nice hot meal and then another and possibly a third entrée for myself was very close.

We'd been told by numerous sources back in Terrace that the Cedarvale Grill would take care of our big appetites.

I stood over my handlebars and shook my head. One little detail we'd overlooked. Had we bypassed the grill with our museum adventure detour? Was it back toward Terrace or just around the bend in front of us?

"Flip a coin?" Beth said.

"Where we going?" Enzo asked, wanting motion of any kind after all that slogging through mud on foot.

"Insane," I said. "We're going insane."

Quinn liked that one. He likes puns and knock-knock jokes these days as well. As much as it pained me, I turned us south.

"The way our luck is running . . ."

Beth nodded. Cover our bases.

We topped the first hill.

"I see it," Enzo called out.

There was nothing but hills and fence line ahead of us. He needed food more than the rest of us if he was hallucinating restaurants.

"Not that way. Behind us."

A few hills to the north loomed a large billboard-type sign. Far enough away that the naked eye couldn't make out the lettering. I called for Beth's bird-watching binoculars. Surprisingly, she did not drop her bike and come running over with them, head bowed geisha-girl-style. Instead, Beth focused them for herself. We waited a few moments for the verdict.

"Cedarvale Grill. Definitely. Written in a sports pub font. The way Cheers looked on the television series."

There was much rejoicing.

I couldn't reach back far enough to high-five Enzo on the Trail-A-Bike, but dismounting the massive rig seemed like too much effort, so I high-fived Quinn, then asked him to pass it on to his little brother for me.

We pedaled with renewed vigor, singing a song made up on the spot about the Cedarvale Grill, to the melody of "Big Rock Candy Mountain." Or that might have been what was going on inside my head; things got fuzzy on the sprint in. Like a horse smelling the barn I was down to instinct for the last push. When we wheeled into the gravel lot there were two cars out front. A damn good sign. By the time we'd parked the rigs and were stowing away the last of our raingear, grabbing dry stuff to change into after we ordered, the door opened slightly to expel an elderly couple. They made their way gingerly down a rather steep set of stairs with a suspect railing. Termites, dry rot of some sort. I took the steps two at a time, to hell with safety, I had bigger problems; namely, that the woman was locking the door and yes, now she was turning the sign over from OPEN to CLOSED.

My shoulders sagging, I turned to face the family. Beth gave me a look, the only one I needed at that moment. It was filled with incredulity that I was walking without a fight. Wet, cold, hungry. This was one worth picking. In that look I saw a montage of moments from our life together, times that have made Beth cringe in the face of confrontations, but often happy with the results.

That look said, "Since when did you take no for answer? After I stood in solidarity when you got us back on a Southwest flight that it was clearly your fault for deplaning in a connecting city five days before. I've seen you charm a movie theater owner into offering you free passes for life, for life . . . just because he thought it was so much fun shooting the shit with you. He wanted you hanging around, maybe drawing a crowd and business. We've been on press junkets you had no business writing about. What do you possibly know about fashion and facials in Maui, knifefire dancing, and the island nation of Yap? A traveling production of *Cats*? Free backstage passes to concerts sold out for months, and what about the time you talked us, a couple of city kids, into a job caretaking a ranch and garden when we had something of the Midas Touch for killing every plant in our care.[138] One closed door and you fold? Where have you taken my real husband?"

I turned, smiled, tried the knob with one hand—knowing it was locked, but this allowed for a look of mock surprise—and held the other hand up in the universal sign for *just one moment of your time, kind lady*. I saw her hesitate, thinking it over. I steepled my hands as if praying. I channeled the light, warmth, optimism, and sincerity of every traveling salesman throughout history.

She brushed away a few strains of her long, graying hair, reminding me of a wildflower late in the season. She wiped her hands on an apron, hesitated a little longer, then unlocked the door.

It was all I needed.

While I never actually put my foot in the doorway, this aging earth

138. Sometimes the excitable boy in Joe serves us no good. When a jack donkey of a guy tossed my son's skoot off the sidewalk with malice—I mean threw a child's first bike for distance—Joe stormed out of the front door and opened up a can of verbal whoop-ass. Ending with, "Every time you break a well-made toy from Scandinavia, another Wal-Mart executive earns his wings and stock options." He ran as Joe approached, literally ran—my boys were watching. I know, I could sell tickets to this marriage.

mother didn't stand a chance. I weaved a narrative that put her under; within minutes the woman was making sure the boys didn't hurt themselves on the way up four rather questionable stairs. Wendy even took Beth's pannier, though she was so slight, I feared it would send her backward down the steps.

Once inside I couldn't help myself. I gave Wendy a hug as if reuniting with a favorite relative. I was a little thrown. This was what real gratitude felt like. I wasn't selling anything. It was a little like pressurizing a plane too quickly—I had to recalibrate.

Much later, when Beth was helping Wendy peel dozens of apples in a cluttered kitchen to the sounds of Joni Mitchell, she would intimate that the only reason she'd opened back up "was because your husband was so well spoken—we don't get that level of articulation around here—and he needed me, not for himself, but to feed his family."[139]

"Oh, he wanted to feed himself," Beth almost added. "We were his ticket in."

"And he has kind eyes." Wendy said.

"Kinda blue," Beth whispered into my ear. This was much later, wrapped close in our sleeping bags on the floor of Wendy's dining room.

"Soulful. She forgot to add something about how soulful my eyes are," I whispered back.

But I'm getting ahead of myself several times over. There's still homemade bubble tea, the looming threat of foreclosure, a grizzly bear family encounter, light snow flurries, a car ride sans car seat or most of

___

139. Yeah, that's my man—a regular Les Misérables moment. You didn't see the big guy pushing away any of the food you put in front of us.

the floorboards, a tour of totems and carvings in an eerie, First Nation village, vacant but for some smoke coming out of a chimney, the burning of dessert, a large make-or-break business luncheon to prepare for, a home makeover restaurant edition—all this before Beth and Wendy peeled their first apple together.

When she opened that door, Wendy wasn't serving her last customers of the day but observing a ritual of hospitality both ancient and universal. By taking in the travelers on her doorstep—when she was in no position to care for anyone—Wendy demonstrated a depth of humanity, a thawing of the coldness lurking in all our DNA. While I initiated her kindness by ignoring a CLOSED sign, Wendy took over as though she was born to it.

The first indication we were in good hands was the liquid ambrosia that followed my offhanded, almost joking inquiry about iced chai. It arrived in a metal milk shake container, unorthodox but bubbling with mint in perfect proportion to the sugar, milk, and ice. This was the tea I'd searched for on five continents.

As we ordered a late lunch, the formalities of hostess and customers fell by the wayside. Wendy lowered her guard with every enthusiastic inquiry about her life and times. I'm a talker by nature, but I'm also a two-way street when it comes to socializing—I listen and retain what's said, play with it for common ground, some spark of humor or a path yet to be chosen by the speaker, then kick it back at them for more.

What started out with Wendy saying she didn't have mac-and-cheese on the menu ended with her sitting with us in the booth, a massive bowl of cheesy noodles placed family-style in the center of the table. Before the boy's plates could run low she'd spoon them full again without missing a beat.

We relaxed. Warmed by the hot meals we started joking, forming an unforced connection with this eclectic woman whose life story was an epic of love and loss, an emotional road map of hope and ruin, much like the hills we'd tackled that day.

Her restaurant was certainly in ruins, or at the very least an extreme state of disrepair. It had nice bones, give it that, checkered title floors and original, kelly-green upholstered booths, a killer counter running the length of the place, the type that begs for regulars parked at it, but clearly the health department hadn't gotten north of Terrace in some time. More than that, though, the Cedarvale Grill felt half finished, nearly packed up for a quick getaway or not fully unpacked, as if the owner knew it could be temporary.

But the food . . . Polishing off slices of homemade berry pie à la mode, I noted out loud that we were in the presence of a gifted baker.

"You're not the first to say so," Wendy said. "I wish it were enough. To love what you do." I thought she was going to cry. "But it's hard . . . to feel inspired when they're about to take it all away."

A familiar story: the artist broken by the business of trying to make what you love pay. I felt like crying with her. But then I'd be shedding a tear or two for myself in the bargain.

What's more, no one—not history, the market, the creative powers of the universe—cares that you're trying to leave a mark, connect with something infinite, help others to see their souls on the canvas, within the chords, and across the pages—until you do, and by then you'll probably be dead. In the end you wipe your face dry and do what you love despite the odds and your own shortcomings.

"Another bill collector comes through that door I swear I might fillet him."

Maybe there was still some fight left in Wendy the Wildflower.

I asked if the piles of papers in the back booth was some sort of mad-genius filing system. She couldn't bring herself to turn around and look at the tsunami of envelopes, receipts, and paper scraps.

"It's why I was closing up early today."

We waited her out.

"I thought maybe there was a sweepstakes check hiding in the debris."

Laughter filled our booth, Wendy included. You could almost see some of the tension leaving her body.

"And there's something else," she said. "I must be crazy, but I'm hosting this big luncheon of the county's business leaders. The banker threatening to shut me out will be here. I was closing early with the pipe dream I could get this place whipped into shape, food prepared for twenty-five, and wow them enough to buy me time. Word of mouth might send folks over here often enough to make a go of the place, or keep it floating until I can sell it."

Now I knew what a proper confession to desperation sounded like.

Looking around the place, with its tables and chairs stacked every which way in the side dining room, art supplies leaning against bags of rice, mops inside planters that once held the expectation of being full of flowers by now, I didn't see how she could pull it off by herself.

"At least the toilet makes funny sounds when you flush it," Enzo said. He meant this as a compliment, like when a kid says, "I like the way Uncle Albert's bald head shines in the sun like a bowling ball," but it made Wendy sigh and slouch.

"I don't know what I was thinking."

I looked at Beth, using the visual shorthand of seventeen years together, clasped my hands, and turned back to Wendy with a devilish grin.[140]

"We're gonna help you make this happen."

An hour before, I couldn't find the strength to climb down off my bicycle and give my son a high-five; now we were gonna take on a rehab project. A Hansel-and-Gretel fixer-upper cottage makeover actually, with less than twenty-four hours before the judges showed up.

This could be fun.

Wendy insisted that we take her car and check out the totems and artwork at the First Nation village a few miles up a side road. She'd have a light dinner of salmon, rice, and vegetables ready when we came back. She said she wanted to use the time to decide a few things.

Before we pulled out of the lot in her rust-bucket, taped-together

---

140. About the hooligan mischief Joe's always getting us into. The truth is, I'm often the one who eggs him on.

Bronco, I leaned out the window. She was standing on her wobbly stoop, fronting a brave smile.

I mouthed, "Let us help you . . . Please."

Dinner sealed the deal. Even the peach cobbler that Wendy kept apologizing for—overcooked because we were laughing so hard at dinner—was heaven. We had to keep this woman cooking, at least through her big luncheon. If it wasn't enough to get her over the hump, we'd see to it that Wendy went down fighting in a spit-shined little eatery in the North Woods.

Beth rode shotgun on our hostess in the kitchen while I put myself to work rejuvenating someone else's worn and weary dream.

The boys arranged furniture under my instruction, sorted silverware, and unpacked long-forgotten appliances. Armed with mops, all of us danced to some old Lovin' Spoonful tunes as we swabbed the decks from end to end.

"This is really nice artwork," I announced. Not that I was a collector, but to me it was original and arresting and had no business stacked behind a sideboard.

"My son did those."

I waited to hear what she wanted to say next. She waited to see if I was really interested. I set down the hammer and took a seat beside the paintings.

"He was here with me for a while, but my sons are a little lost to me these days. Both are somewhere in the States right now. The painter"—she head nodded at the canvases—"was using my dining room as a studio and helping around the grill when he felt like it, but it got too hard to do both and see me floundering with bills."

I give her a wistful nod. We're both parents.

"I don't think the paint fumes were helping business, either."

She took another look at the work, a mother's love washing over her face, but you could see Wendy the person thought he had real talent.

"He did that rooster for me. The model for it lived out back until something ate it."

I held the painting to the light. There was an empty chicken coop near the toolshed. Something ate all of them.

"Hey, those are really good."

Beth was out of the kitchen, checking why Wendy was so long with a load of carrots. If my wife praised a piece of art it meant something. Beth's own mom struggled to make a living, but after her death a retrospective exhibit of her work was held in Santa Fe, New Mexico. The woman had the touch—weaving, painting, found art, jewelry. Everything she crafted, including her children, became works of art. Her own life was an unfinished one in progress that she got called away from too soon. But the walls of our house and of Beth's siblings showcase her legacy. We'd rather have her. The art feels like an echo . . . a window between us and wherever she went.

"You've got to hang these," Beth said. "They make the room come to life."[141]

---

141. For a very long time I couldn't look at certain paintings my mom did. We had a complicated relationship and a chaotic family life. I raised myself mostly and we all helped raise my mom. But when it's all you have left of a person . . . Joe hung the stuff all over our house without asking me. I took it all down once but put it back up before he got home. My children's own artwork now hangs beside the art of a grandmother they never met. Together like that, I love it.

I already had the rooster centered along the back wall.

Wendy seemed to find a second wind after that.

As dusk set in, I asked our hostess where to pitch the tents. She showed me the high spot on the lawn. Putting in the final stakes, I felt rain begin to fall.

Though I hadn't seen any lightning, a growl of thunder sounded close, as in, over my shoulder.

It's not every day I mistake a grizzly bear for weather. There, poking his nose out of the woods ten yards behind me. I calmly worked my way around to the other side of the tent.

Three bear cubs and another adult emerged from the darkening forest coverage.

They walked straight at the tent. Not a charge, just a steady gait that I took as a cue to retreat. Slowly backing away to the steps. The bears ignored me completely, but the tent caught their attention. Fortunately, I hadn't tossed in any panniers with food smells from the bikes yet. I was planning to put those inside the restaurant.

The tent happened to be in their path. They stopped to sniff and ponder blue blobs on their way to the river. I looked back to the large windows of the grill. Beth, Wendy, and the boys were gathered, watching. As these massive creatures crossed the highway, the misting rain changed to light snow flurries. It melted as soon as it hit the pavement but stayed a little longer on the backs of the bears. They waited there awhile, maybe enjoying the flakes on their fur. I stood, letting some flakes land on my face. At least once, everyone should feel snow touch them on the first day of fall.

In the time it took to go into the restaurant we were back to rain, coming down hard and fast.

"I don't know what I was thinking," Wendy said. "That's where the animals walk to get to the river. You guys can sleep in here as long as you don't mind laying your bags out on the floor."

I thought about tearing the tents down or pulling them around back where the bikes were stashed under tarps, but I'd only succeed in drenching myself. Once a tent is in a downpour it's best to leave it standing. The morning sun dries it in minutes.

While working off months of grime from the counters and mirrors, I eavesdropped on the girls.

"He came here running from the draft." Talking about her husband. "We lived on Salt Spring Island, where you guys had all that fun. It's a magic place. Those were our best years."

Beth asked what ended it.

"Nothing. The accumulated weight of nothing. Art was a man without a country, or that's how he justified moving around so much. He'd come and go until he stayed away for good. We were always sort of in-between together anyway, but I didn't mind that feeling until he wanted to take the boys with him down south."

I leaned in closer to the swinging door to hear better.

"So the boys moved here with you?"

"For a while it was working. Then they stopped running the bus to the school fifty kilometers away. And my help moved on and the kids felt trapped. I have a sixteen-year-old son living with friends in Smithers now. Close to his school and friends. I didn't want it this way but I was starting to worry that one day he'd just get into a car with a customer passing through. He was that ready to go. This way I know there's a roof over his head."

I heard cutlery set down. Beth was hugging her. It was like I could see through walls.

"My husband, he was far from perfect. I stopped wanting him back a long time ago. But . . . it's hard when everyone leaves."

It was quiet.

"People leave for their own reasons . . . you shouldn't feel like it's all on you," Beth said.

I stepped away from the door. As I cleaned I couldn't shake Beth's words. Every relationship rides off the rails at some point. Nothing big, fast, and worth getting behind stays the course. With people, it has to do with bringing two sets of chemicals close like that for long periods of time. Our toddler put it best. "People go boom."

We went boom, mostly because I was playing the role of parent when Beth had been raised once already. She wanted risk and passion and someone who would let her take chances when all I seemed to be about was giving her instructions and something that looked like safe passage.

Beth had her reasons, but she didn't leave.

We tore it down together. Now we're trying to build something better . . . each of us adding our own parts. It feels like it anyway.

On the back end of our rough patch Beth gave me a no-particular-occasion greeting card. I found it in my bag while driving up to an event in Seattle. Blank inside so she could put it in her own words.

"Give me your Forever . . . not a day less will do."

That card and some water, and I could hold out until the sun folded in on itself.

I saw the bears coming back across the road. Risk and passion. Definitely in the mix these days.

Beth came out of the kitchen. I pointed out the bear family.

"It's like a grizzly bear version of us," I said.

Beth hugged me from behind. To think I almost lost her.

"Wendy's a bit of a train wreck," she said.

I nodded.

"I like her," Beth said.

We got maybe four hours of sleep, what with all the activity going on in the kitchen. Wendy had a little bedroom in back, but it's doubtful she slept for more than an hour or two. We heard her as she cooked and prepped and banged around in there until the early-morning hours. Beth hung in with her until nearly midnight.

Over the fruit-filled crêpes she served us for breakfast I put the question to her.

"How much sleep do you get a night?"

She waved me off. "I can't remember the last time I got more than three hours straight."

I had second thoughts about the wisdom of helping her salvage her business. Sisyphus pushing the same rock up the hill came to mind.

"Restaurant owners don't sleep," She gave me a weak smile. I could see an aging beauty underneath all that flour, given some real rest and a shower.

"The toilet's not as fun anymore," Enzo said, disappointment lacing his voice.

I smiled at Wendy.

After breakfast I tackled the patio, yard, and steps. If nothing else, a community leader would not break a hip stumbling off the stoop that day. Quinn made a real find just when I thought no more could be done to face-lift the grill's facade.

"Look, Christmas blinkers and plastic chile pepper lights."

Placing myself in some peril, I managed to balance several chairs atop one another to string the lights and peppers in a festive showing of cheer and resolve.

Wendy wasn't just open for business; those peppers, along with a stable set of steps, dinosaur toys along the railing, and blinking holiday lights announced, *We're staying in business, come on in!*

Wendy loaded us down with goodies, a dozen hard-boiled eggs in a ziplock bag—beginning a morning tradition of boiling up portable protein for the road from there through Nova Scotia—a couple dozen to-die-for cinnamon rolls (which we managed to consume in under two days), leftover crêpes, and the recipe for that iced chai.

All that was left to do was say our good-byes and retrieve my waterproof sealskin socks. I'd been drying them on the middle rack of the oven. Wendy was right. Cook 'em at 350 for fifteen minutes, then flip 'em. They'd dry, but not catch fire. Let's keep that recipe in the family, shall we? Less the health department knows, the better.

I took one last look. The dining room was set for a holiday feast. Every table had a centerpiece courtesy of Beth, clean silver, and cloth napkins. And Beth called it: The artwork made the room.

Beth wrote our address on an envelope and made Wendy promise to give us a full report and contact information when and if she found herself somewhere else in the world beside the grill.

She watched us assume our positions on the bikes.

"Quite a family," Wendy said. "You've given me back so much."

I noticed she'd changed into a somewhat less stained blouse and brighter-colored Birkenstocks. One more round of hugs and we were off.

I stopped us at the top of the hill. Wendy was gone but it was nice to look into her valley one more time. Even if the dream wasn't going according to plan, I could see why she'd come.

"Eagle," Enzo announced. We watched it ride the thermals for a while.

Beth rolled up to me.

"You think we did any good?"

I nodded. "Feels like it."

Had we done enough to be the difference? To bring home a tidy, happy ending after the commercial break? Probably not. But all of us, Wendy included, had come to life down there and pulled together for a time.[142]

If there's more to it than that, I haven't found it.

---

142. In typical Wendy fashion, she did mail a card using my envelope but she left some things out. It featured a grizzly bear photo on the front, which I thought was clever. No return address on the outside. We hovered around the dining room table, expectations high. Joe opened the card. "Love, Wendy" was all she'd written. No one said anything, then Joe started laughing. Then we were all laughing. She was letting us decide how it ended.

Chapter 22

It's Best You Don't Know About These Things

I never think of the future—it comes soon enough.
—Albert Einstein

Back on Salt Spring Island, our cycling friend Steve Pal, the one who so desperately wanted to join the cause, had slipped me a book—*Cycling Canada* or something like that. We lost the cover, so I can't be sure. He patted the spot in my jersey pocket where he'd put it and offered a solemn nod, as if passing me the Good Book, a treasure map, or a tome full of his family's best recipes. It was a no-nonsense guide covering routes from his home base of Vancouver Island to Jasper National Park. While it listed a few attractions and offered occasional descriptions of amenities, it was also the most angry rant disguised as a

guidebook I've ever come across—everything was subservient to the explanation of all elevation changes and mileage. There were a few asides about plant species but mostly the elevation and mileage were what mattered to him. Every cyclist likes to bemoan tough hills and headwinds, but this guy wrote as if he'd been forced across Canada by bike to save his family, being held hostage on the other end by a small-press publisher.

"Ride every mile, write the book, then we'll see about your family."

We didn't use it in the way it was traditionally designed (and not as toilet paper or firestarter). Truth being, I don't like to know what's ahead of me. If someone tells me, there's nothing I can do about it, but for the most part, surprise me. That's sacrilege to plotters, planners, and the entire population of engineers out there, but it would break my heart if all the turns, climbs, distances, and challenges were given to us in advance. A cheat sheet. If we were locked in on where we'd sleep and eat, how far we'd get each day, and who we'd be staying with for the length of Canada, you'd find me rocking quietly in a corner telling whoever would listen to "Make the big, mean anal-retentive cartographers and their overly helpful travel agent friends go away."

Reservations are for people on business trips and two weeks of vacation per year. We're on an adventure here, folks.

So the book was poison, really. Except when read as an epilogue, a palate cleanser, a postscript. We'd break it out and read aloud the pages covering the day we'd just experienced; a cheap, satisfying form of entertainment. Discussion sprang up over things the author left out; we'd concur with him in places and laugh when he wrote with that personally offended tone about rough, steep, or winding roads. And here we

thought experiencing all the contours of a country was the general idea of a bike ride. I hope his family survived. It was great, though, to have names to put to the less familiar plants and trees we were camping around. A useful book, but there was absolutely no temptation to read ahead and ruin the uncertainty of another day.

Those rollers into Cedarvale had clocked in at ninety kilometers according to the angry book. Then the Wendy rehab experience and precious little sleep had left us on questionable legs. In our favor: weeks of on-the-job training atop bikes. The road map showed us doing roughly 70k into New Hazleton. I looked away, but I wasn't fast enough. The red line on the map to New Hazleton could have doubled as a seismograph during an earthquake. When cheap road maps draw in big curves, it's not a good sign. Even this glimpse was too much information. As it turns out, I can't handle the truth. Fortunately, I'm easily distracted. The countryside was breathtaking—pedaling as we were through wide valley-bottom farmland. A colossal climb out of one post-

card, up and up and up some more, then down into another valley of kelly-green grass or tall corn about to come in for the harvest. These farms were so remote and quaint you'd swear you were coasting through a painting. The air might have been the cleanest I'd taken in since looping around New Zealand. I breathed deep and savored, and prepared for the next climb. We were shelling and eating hard-boiled eggs in such quantities on the fly that my cholesterol, tested at that moment, would have been a cautionary tale. But anything to keep the engine burning hot and fast. The boys discussed Nerf guns with the intensity of PhD candidates and categorized their favorite waterslide parks along the route. I appreciated their chatter. We'd found "the zone," the place on a ride that brings you back for the next one, and no amount of hills or sore legs could pull us out of it. When a climb did break us, we'd dismount with hardly a word, push the final hundred feet, saddle back up, and roll on; nothing but a thing.

We didn't make New Hazleton that day, so South Hazleton had to do. It was close, but my legs cried *no mas* as we topped a long slight grade late in the afternoon. A sign pointing to tent camping, RVs, and cabins pulled me like a magnet to the left. I took the turn without asking Beth.

We'd eaten our way through our supplies, but the campground store had boxed chow. It would have to do. A woman shaped like a barrel of Booker Noe whiskey waited at the register, while I tried to make my selections. It wasn't going so well. I seemed to be stumped by the pasta choices, or possibly I'd nodded off for a moment leaning against the shelving. I pulled myself together long enough to ask the barrel lady if there were any such thing as microwavable boxed pastas.

She smiled, waddled over, and picked me out a nice selection of empty calories for the boys.

"Any . . . any chance you have a microwave I could borrow?"

A blind man could see the three-foot-wide dinosaur of a microwave on a shelf behind her, clearly labeled, EMPLOYEES ONLY.

"Oh, sweetie, you look plumb worn out. I saw the monstrosity you pedaled in on." She shook her head and came around the counter once more. "Why don't you take a load off? I'll get these dishes heated up for you."

I mumbled my thanks and went looking for a chair in the back of the store. She found me laid out in a pile of dry goods—bags of flour and rice that hadn't made it on the shelves yet. I was curled up in a little ball, the late-afternoon sun drying some of my sweat-soaked jersey. I was dreaming about sleep.

"Listen, sweetie. You've got yourselves camped out, and maybe you're set on that, but for seven more dollars, you can have beds."

Disoriented, my cheek covered in unbleached flour, I came to long enough to hand over a ten-spot and accept a key. I had no idea whether it was to a car I'd just won or would open the city. She took further pity and carried the pasta dinners to the cabin.

Beth watched me enter a cabin, following a three-hundred-pound woman carrying food. That this seemed par for the course meant we'd brought Beth completely over to the ways of the road.

Later, when I came around again, Beth was sitting on the other bed, the one all three of my sons were not jumping on. They saved that treat for the one I had passed out across. Just as well; if I needed anything more than I needed sleep, it was food. I found chunks of Wendy's

cinnamon rolls and used them to wipe up orphaned pasta hiding in the trays.

I curled up again at Beth's feet.

"Baby, maybe I'm coming down with some rare disease. I've never jumped off my tracks this hard after, what, fifty miles."

Beth smiled. She was holding the *Cycling Canada* book. Clearing her throat in a theatrical way, she began: "Today will be your hardest of the ride so far. It may well be your most difficult along the entirety of the Yellowhead Highway."

From there he waxed excessive about pitches, elevation gains and losses, grades, asphalt textures (really? you're blaming the pavement now?), and unpredictable winds through the passes. But one look at that day's topo map would have sent weaker souls screaming from the building.

And that's why I don't read ahead. By knowing the score after the damage is done I get to sit, or in this case curl up in the fetal position, with a satisfied smile for a job well done, or at the very least all done. I didn't fret the "hardest day" on the Yellowhead. In fact, I was feeling better already, knowing I wasn't dying of a rare blood disorder.

"How you holding up, baby?" I asked.[143]

"Glad to be sleeping in a bed and not Wendy's floor."

I had a feeling she wanted to say something else.

"What?"

She closed the book. "I'm pretty rough, too . . . after a day like today, so I can't imagine how you feel. It's been too long since we slept

143. I was wiped out, too, but someone had to stay awake until the kids went to bed.

late in the morning. New Hazleton's 10k from here. What say we get a late start and find some hiking trails in New Hazleton? Work some different muscles. Let the boys run wild for more than twenty minutes at a time."

"Sounds . . . like . . . a . . . plan."

I don't remember moving back to my own bed, but when I woke up in it, I was nearly healed . . . and hungry enough to eat the furniture.

New day, new game, new rules. Today, we'd feel the ground under our feet . . .

Chapter 23

Yellowhead Highway Trivia for a Hundred, Alex

Two things are infinite: the universe and human stupidity; and I'm not sure about the universe.

—Albert Einstein

Some trivia that kept us intrigued for hundreds of miles: Why was it called the Yellowhead Highway? The answer might have been locked away in the *Cycling Canada* guidebook, but, between rants and flora lessons, he hadn't mentioned it yet, and I wasn't reading ahead.

As good detectives, it's not as if we'd been sitting on our hands. The boys launched a formal inquiry outside a sporting goods store in Prince Rupert, but so far answers ranged from "Who cares" to "Nobody's ever asked" to "Are you asking me because you know or because you don't know?"[144]

It became an inside joke. The boys were keeping track, and by Cedarvale seventy people living and working along it didn't know why it was called the Yellowhead Highway, or how it got that name.

"A lot of yellow flowers along it?"

Don't think so.

"That yellow strip running down the middle of it."

That isn't even an answer, really.

"It's shaped like a head if you look at the map?"

No it isn't, even when Enzo rotated the map around three times.

"Is that what it's called? We say, 'Get on the main road and turn at this farm or that store.' "

While we appreciated the Forrest-Gump-like quality of that contribution, we found our answer at a welcome center on the outskirts of New Hazleton. Not only the answer but a twenty-foot-tall monument commemorating it. Here's what we learned.

It was named after fair-haired Pierre Bostonais (nicknamed Tête Jaune, French for "Yellow Head"), an Iroquois-Métis trapper employed as a guide by the Hudson's Bay Company. Bostonais led one of the first expeditions for the company to the interior of BC through the pass in 1820. The First Nation people were taken by his light hair, since they

---

144. It was like not knowing the name of the street you live on.

hadn't seen anything like it before. The road carved by his route became known as the Yellowhead because natives began referring to it this way.

Ah . . . solving the mystery of the Yellowhead was like scratching an itch. We felt giddy, relieved, satisfied. We posed in front of the statute and clowned around.

I went inside the center to get some dining recommendations.

"I can hand you this list of restaurants, but we are not allowed to pick one place over another," said the girl behind the counter. Her level of enthusiasm told me this was the only summer job left or court-appointed community service.

"Okay, but come on, where should we eat?"

She gave me a blank stare.

I picked up the list. Just names, nothing else, not even categories. "Where do you eat?"

She looked around for help. The older lady yawned.

"I kinda hate this job," she said, taking back the list.

The older woman stepped to the counter. "It's on account some of the eateries were paying off previous visitor's center workers to send them customers. I'll say this much, one place in town has really, really good food."

I smiled. "But you're not gonna tell me?"

"I wouldn't tell you if you were Pierre Bostonais himself."

"Who?" the girl asked.

This was too good to pass up. I turned back to her.

"Why do they call it the Yellowhead Highway, anyway?"

She looked like she wanted to be somewhere else. "No idea. But if it helps, Pierre should not eat at the Chinese restaurant."

The older lady gave the girl a look. "What? I didn't tell *him* where not to eat."

I pushed off the counter. My work was done.

"It's okay, Pierre hasn't been hungry in a long time," I said.

Beth wanted to know what was going on in there.

"Visitor's center staff doesn't know why it's called the Yellowhead Highway."

I pointed at the twenty-foot-tall statute and shrugged. Our inside joke just got funnier.

"Oh, and I think our best bet is the fruit stand over there. Restaurant recommendations are verboten around here."

Chapter 24

Climate-Controlled Living

We planned to sleep outside but a hotel billing itself as the "only place in town with air-conditioning" proved too quirky to pass up. It was sixty degrees when we pulled up. They run hot-blooded in Hazleton.

When the clerk suggested we lock our bikes inside the storeroom beside kegs of beer, I felt we'd made the right decision. Enzo mistook the frosty mug of booze being held by a bear on the marquee for a root beer float. When he told her, our waitress made root beer floats on the house, "For tickling my funny bone, young man." Nobody was stand-

ing on formalities around there.

"Which bone is that?" Enzo whispered. "Because I didn't touch her."

In Prince George we hunkered down for a few hours in the home of an excellent children's book author, Richard Thompson. The boys had read him and felt like we were in the home of royalty. In fact, it was the home we always wanted to create for our kids. Everything was color and light and whimsy. The piano bench was shellacked with note music, there was folk art everywhere, and the family had given up their theme beds so that we could get some rest in style before boarding a train in the wee hours of the next morning. Thompson, as well as being a great writer and a good father, was a touring cyclist. With his wife and daughter, he recounted their adventures together while we ate the homemade hotcakes and hand-cut fruit salad they'd gotten up at 5 AM to fix for us.

What alternate universe of nice had these people come from? I wanted to stay longer and get to know them better.

The boys were just as stunned that people lived this way. The table was shaped like a cow, the coffee table another barnyard animal. In a house that looked like the set from a Technicolor cartoon, these people got up in the middle of the night to feed their guests before arranging a taxi to take us to the train station.

We didn't want to have to take the train, but we'd been warned by everyone there was a two-hundred-kilometer patch of hard riding with no services. Surprisingly, angry author from the guidebook made no mention of it. Probably because the kidnappers told him he had to

pedal every mile.

Richard smiled in his rainbow-colored suspenders.

"It should be another adventure, riding on the train. Have the boys been on a train before?"

Good question.

"Boys, have you been on a train before?"

Since it was their first ride on the rails, I got to see it through fresh eyes. For the first few hours what I saw was excitement, novelty, and interest, a chance to relax and watch the countryside we would have cycled through. After that Matteo started looking for stuff to throw, which he could do with abandon in the campgrounds. The older boys searched around for somewhere to run or something to climb, but that was difficult inside a long cylinder. When they ran out of card games, Enzo asked if we could open the windows of the train. Get some wind on our faces. I wondered if we'd made the right decision. That's when Beth mouthed to me from across the aisle, "I wish we were on our bikes."

Lessons learned: A lot of great songs have been written about train travel, but my family will take a bike ride over a good melody and catchy lyrics any day.

Chapter 25

The Gatekeepers of Jasper Park

I have a kingdom but no home, and that's fine by me.
—Anonymous

Enzo rang his bell, but the billy goats took no notice. He rang it some more just because he loves making noise at any hour of the day. We're the loudest family in the history of the world. I've tested this by closing my eyes and listening in restaurants, bathrooms, and hotel lobbies around the globe. Without fail I hear my children rise above the din.

How three boys can sound like an entire bar of New Year's Eve revelers is beyond us.[145]

The goats were packed in on the highway like New York subway commuters, chomping the grass growing up between the cracks. Our big bicycle spooked none of them. When animals herd together in these numbers it takes a lot to get them to stampede. We were cut off by the river of animals, as were a line of tourists in cars behind us. It seemed like a natural moment to break for lunch, climb boulders, and try to commune with the goats that wandered over to check us out. One tried chewing on Beth's panniers, but lost interest.

"It's the Yellowhead Highway salad bar," Quinn said. "For goats."

We'd reached the point in our adventure where our actions were like water, no longer pushing against anything. An average day on the Yellowhead threw any combination of hail, humidity, bears, sun, 10 percent grades, or grasshoppers in your direction . . . and that was just before lunch. Adapt or go home. Water was the right form to take. Most of our bodies are that anyway; it was just a matter of shape-shifting our attitudes.

Traffic was backed up for a mile beyond the curve.

It makes you wonder, when folks on vacation feel the need to rev, yell, and actually try to ram the goats in their quest to get to a national park, a scenic area, where they hope to kick back and admire, among other things . . . billy goats.

145. It's the one thing about having all boys that I was not prepared for, the volume. I once told Joe, only half joking, that sometimes I daydream about going deaf—Joe suggested a small industrial accident that would render us both temporarily deaf or very hard of hearing, for about the next eighteen years. It would lift like a spell in fairy tales: The playing of "Pomp and Circumstance" and our sons walking across a stage to accept their diplomas would trigger a complete recovery.

"Technically, I think those are big-horned sheep," Beth said.

"No less admirable," I said. It's a critical mass event, big-horned style.

Someone behind us had had enough. He stood in the bed of his truck and shot a few rounds from a hunting rifle into the air.

The sheep didn't yield any real estate. I worried this might turn into the livestock version of the LA Riots.

Of course the shooter's license plate was from the good old US of A.

"You sheared sheep in New Zealand," Beth said. "What did they do to get them off the roads down there?"

"You'd wait," I said. "Maybe that's why there's a pub every ten miles or so down there. Plus they weren't big-horned bad boys eating grass growing up through the cracked roadway. They wandered off on their own."

Beth shrugged and went back to lounging among the wild-flowers.[146]

It took an honest-to-goodness cowboy type to uncork the roadway. He strolled up in the outfit, only it wasn't an outfit if he wore it all the time. I guess they're just called clothes, then. Two Border collies ran beside him. When he was about a hundred feet from the mass of ani-mals, he whistled a few times and the collies went to work.

It was something to see, but you had to keep watching because it was over so fast. The cowboy disappeared, the traffic barreled ahead, but we held off a little longer, until the road was empty again.

I saw Beth shaking her head as she pulled her bike upright.

"What?"

---

146. It was a perfect afternoon. I needed nothing else in my life at that moment but that field and those bighorns and my family enjoying themselves with me.

She smiled wistfully. "I was wondering how long it will take after our trip is over before, you know, we turn back into them."

I thought it over. "I can promise you I'll never be the a-hole with the shotgun."

She nodded. "But you know what I mean."

I did. It was the Gordian knot of my life that I desperately wanted to untangle once and for all.

"Moving to the country, gonna eat me a lot of peaches," I sang.

Beth said, "Just say when."

She pushed off toward Jasper. I knew she meant it. Beth needs so little to be happy. The miles together had shown me it wasn't a brave front she put up, or a time-out-of-mind road trip she'd tricked her brain into enduring. I'd married a pioneer of the highest order.[147]

It wasn't the when, but the how of it that kept me up nights.

Parts of what we wanted would shake out while other things got hopelessly tied. As we rode away I noticed some sheep coming back onto the road behind us. They knew where they wanted to go, even when forces beyond their control tried to push them aside. They just came at it from another direction.

"We should be like the sheep, honey."

Beth laughed. "I thought that was the problem."

"Not regular sheep, Jasper big-horned sheep."

She thought it over. "Maybe the sheep *will* inherit the earth."

As I passed my favorite pioneer I said, "Trust me, in New Zealand, they already have."

147. Giddyap.

Chapter 26

Jasper Welcoming Committee

In my shoot-from-the-hip style, I had not called ahead to see what activities I could wrangle from Jasper's local business community in return for writing about them in a magazine feature. I hadn't thought about journalism much on this road trip. Yes, *Bicycling* magazine was footing our expenses, and would be waiting for a big spread at the other end. Presumably, I was also gathering research for the next book. It's a trap to head out the door, though, with the thing prepackaged in advance by marketers and product placement whores. And that's coming from a sometimes reformed artiste never very far from the dark side of selling out for the big score.

But when we rolled into Jasper, a playground of outdoor activities,

on a Friday afternoon, I wanted to find someone, anyone I could sell out to: rafting, mountain biking, boat rides to see caribou and icy blues of the glaciers. I had a price and it wasn't very high. In truth I had nothing to trade. I was on assignment, but any journalist claiming they'll get your company into print, regardless of whether it makes sense for the piece, is fooling you, or he has compromising images of the publishers. I would do my best, but I told stories; I didn't push puff pieces or sell advertising in sheep's clothing.

When I made this speech to Debbie, the only person left standing on a Friday afternoon in the chamber of commerce office, she called my honesty refreshing. Plus, she said she knew I was required to make that disclaimer. She winked. I'd tried.

I told her to punch me up on the Internet. Look over my credentials and a few clips and if she still wanted to track down some comped activities for us, the family would be in the lobby thumbing through rack brochures. She came out a few minutes later.

"You and your family are exactly who we want to attract to Jasper. Let me make some calls and see what we can put together at this late hour. Come back by around 5 PM. See if I can pull some rabbits from out of a few hats." She winked again.

We explored the town until quitting time. Debbie had been kind enough to let us store our bikes and gear behind the chamber building. When we came back the place looked closed. Debbie must have struck out or she'd been shining us on long enough to get this grimy vagabond biking family out of her office before the carpet had to be cleaned all over again.

I gave Beth the hey-we-tried shrug, and went around back to

unlock and retrieve our equipment.

Debbie almost knocked me down. She popped out of her basement lair with a stack of papers in her hands.

"I have your whole weekend planned," she said. "There's rafting the Athabasca River with Maligne Rafting Adventures, mountain biking rental from Freewheel Cycles, and we have an excellent boat trip with Maligne Lake Tours to see the glaciers, do some fishing, and photograph wildlife."

She had more activities for us to choose from than we had time to complete.

"You blow a mean horn of plenty around here, Debbie."

Before we rode off to our campground with a three-page itinerary, times, tickets, names, and reservation numbers, Debbie gave the boys lollipops and bear buttons.

"Why haven't you been selling out before now, Dad?" Quinn asked.

Chapter 27

Grumpy Old Man, Part 2

Since the chamber of commerce had come through in a big way, we'd decided to call Jasper Park's South Campground home for a few days, prepaying for three nights since it was the high season. Also, there wasn't a hotel room unrented in the tricounty area. Debbie had checked. I didn't want to worry about losing a spot of ground with bathrooms and showers at the end of our fun-filled days. Besides, Matteo had taken to clawing at the TVs and throwing stuff around the hotel rooms unless we walked him around outside until bed. Barely one and he'd already gone native.

Beth mentioned that I was putting our relative comfort ahead of spontaneity, which meant I should be checked for a fever.

"Prepaid camping from the man who won't read ahead in the guidebook. Careful, you'll wake up one day driving a fifth wheel to KOAs if you're not careful."

I defended myself, pointing out that we'd selected a campground fully ten kilometers south of town.

"We'll still need to pedal to our pick up points and some of our activities. There'll still be suffering."

"Please, 10k is a warm-up." Then she said something that is the equivalent of Spanish fly to a lifelong cyclist. "Let's never be off the bikes as long as we were from Port Hardy to Prince Rupert."

I watched her pop off the pannier like a seasoned biker. We'd created a monster, a beautiful, bike-crazed monster. Everyone was going native on me.

I looked over the itinerary by headlamp. "As a bonus, nothing starts before dawn, so we won't have to ride in the dark."[148]

I'd bought additional lighting for the bikes, but I wasn't eager to test it among the most distracted of drivers in the world, tourists looking for animals or fumbling with maps as they went.

"Check this out." Beth pointed into the shadows of the big trees that ringed our campsite.

Elk were emerging, walking slowly but deliberately in our direction. The boys stopped playing a balance beam game on a log. Beth scooped Matteo up and deposited him into the papoose on her back.

---

148. Aren't you a prince?

The elk kept coming until they were a few yards away. There had to be ten of them, all searching for the mushroom shoots that resided around our tents and peppered the ground in our site. One elk tasted the corner of Beth's tent, but apparently the mushrooms were better, or he was off blue foods.

"They're female elk," Beth whispered. "All of them."

Some of the animals sat down.

"Make yourselves at home, girls," I said. They did.

Within a half an hour, they'd become part of the scenery. We worked around them and they did not make any aggressive moves at us. A ranger swung by.

"I see you've met the herd." He walked up to one and made some clicking noises. The elk looked at him like he was a moron and went back to eating. "We can move you guys to another site if they're a bother."

We took a poll and decided we liked having them around.

The only challenge was that Matteo wanted to pet them.

"They're hiding over here from the males," the ranger said. "It's coming up on the summer rutting season. In a few more days there won't be anywhere those boys can't find 'em, eh?"

"They're like outlaws," Quinn said.

"It's more like boys chase the girls," Beth explained.

Each evening, we'd pedal in from ransacking the tourism industry with our antics to be greeted by the elk and our German pals. Wolfgang and Antje were the most shiny, put-together cyclists I'd ever come across. And they'd had the misfortune to end up camped beside us, a rowdy, unkempt band of Americans. Their outfits matched, their gear was immaculate, they appeared to shower every day. Wolfgang a lawyer from Berlin and Antje worked in his office. They were even the same height, topping out at chest level on me.

To them we must have looked like a family of giant sewer rats, but for some reason they braved the noise and odors, the language barriers and bits of gear spread across not one but two picnic tables, to talk adventures.

He couldn't get over the scope and size of our endeavor.

"You pull this all? You don't have vehicles follow?" he asked. She stood by his side, smiling and waiting for my answer.

Instead, I told a lively, elaborate, and circuitous story involving Beth's jeans and the Harry Potter book battle we waged with each other. I was making a point about how weight mattered, but not more than my family's happiness. "So now I carry the cute jeans and Beth agreed to haul Harry Potter," I ended with.

"Harry Potter?" she asked. Confused.

Wolfgang shook his head.

"Girl's pants . . . he . . . . he's saying he wears the girl's pants for riding."

Then Wolfgang switched over to German. She listened, nodded, frowned. She turned back to me, looking a bit frightened but still trying to smile.

"No girl's pants . . . Nein girl's pants!" I said, shaking my head vigorously. Then I added what I should have opened and closed with. "And no vehicle."

"Ah," they both chimed.

I thought it best to scale back my non sequiturs for the duration of our talks.

His English wasn't bad, it was the speed at which I threw things at him, out of context, that tripped us up.

I slowed down, threading one thought at a time. Wolfgang fell into the flow while Antje continued to nod and smile and understand nothing.

Something we all understood when we arrived back in camp on the third afternoon: Trouble had established a beachhead in the campsite across from us.

They looked all right at first glance. Who were we to throw stones at personal appearances? A thick quilt hung drying between trees. Tents had been opened but not set up yet. One of the two guys, college-aged but currently enrolled in the university of life, sat atop a cooler strumming a guitar, while the other gent, in oversized hiking boots he left untied, stacked entirely too much flammable material into one of the waist-high grills the parks provide for cooking hot dogs and whatnot. We hate these grills because you can't build a proper fellowship fire in one, and our boys are the perfect heights to whack their heads on them.

We watched in growing amazement as the guy balanced wood, cardboard, anything he could find in a complex sculpture atop the grill, opened up a can of fuel, dowsed it liberally, then struck a match.

People back in Jasper could have seen the initial fireball. We could feel the heat from twenty feet away. I had Beth bring the boys close in case we had to make a quick escape.

Wolfgang stopped what he was doing around his grill. They'd established a kitchen area tidy enough to win approval from the health department. He brushed some imaginary crumbs off his table, then came over to our campsite.

"This is verboten?" He nodded over to the bonfire across the path.

"Very," I said.

Wolfgang had seen the same sign at the front gate expressly forbidding fires except for cooking. A flaming branch fell from the side of the gents' grill.[149] They hooted and danced around like a pair of warlocks, kicking the flaming stick against the grill pole then adding more kindling to it so that soon you couldn't tell that there was a grill there at all, just a stalk of fire and enough smoke that the campground could have used a smoke alarm.

I went over to spoil their fun and save the forest from an unprescribed burn.[150]

---

149. They were such true-blue rednecks. God knows where these two were from. I can't imagine they were Canadian. If so they were from the Florida-shaped part of the country.

150. Joe always did have a thing for Smokey Bear. He even worked one winter in Ruidoso—the place that invented the Forest Service campaign icon. This is the same place Joe cleared trail with the smoke jumpers for like I'm guessing two days, making him, in his mind, an honorary smoke jumper, lifetime member.

The guys nodded at me but did nothing to put it out. Guitar Player even tossed on the remaining log in his hand, as if he just couldn't help himself.

"They have no water," Wolfgang noted.

Other campers had arrived tracking the source of the smoke.

I went for the ranger.

An impressive mushroom cloud of gray smoke erupted when the ranger used a water truck's hose to douse the flame. Ash settled over the area like Mount St. Helens. Wolfgang and Antje worked into the evening to restore their gear to showroom-new condition. We used the time to play cards and read another Harry Potter chapter aloud.

Over at Little Appalachia, as we now referred to it, they ate cold hot dogs, drank beer (also verboten in camp), and composed songs about caribou to the Counting Crows tune of "Mr. Jones and Me." Over and over in the wee hours of the morning we heard the same melody, but different lyrics praising the beauty and sweetness of the animals hunkered down near their tents.

"Do you think he knows it's an elk he's serenading?" Beth asked.

"I don't know, but if the Counting Crows knew what he was doing to their music, he'd be facing a lawsuit."

The rednecks caught a second wind around midnight, rekindling a smaller but still impressive fire outside their grill and butchering other folksingers well into the night.

At one point I woke to hear what sounded like bottle rockets going off. I went back to sleep, hoping it was a bad dream.

"You come," Antje urged, pointing over to Little Appalachia. We'd been shuffling through the morning duties of coffee making and hikes to the bathroom when Antje fetched me.

Wolfgang and Beth, with a baby strapped to her back, were already there trying to manage the mayhem, and it was mayhem.

Elk were running everywhere. The males had tracked down their mates and were ready to get it on. Our Canadian rednecks had left hot dogs and marshmallows in the open so the female elk were well into those snacks when the males arrived. Adding to the confusion, one of the two guys had drunk too much to set up his tent in the wee hours, so he'd simply crawled between the tarp and the tent material lying on the ground and called it good. I mistook this for damage the elk had not done.

Guitar Player was in a state, surrounded by sex-starved elk at the start of a frenzy. He probably had good reason to be afraid. But there was no call to swing his guitar at the animals he'd been writing love songs to just hours before.

Beth, towering over Wolfgang by a good foot, did what she could to protect them . . . the animals, that is. Wolfgang, whom I later learned was a champion fencer back in his country, weaved among the excited beasts to extract the guitar from the reeling redneck's grip in one fluid move.

Beth corralled some of the elk away from the marshmallows.[151] But Guitar Plater lost his balance in the mayhem and fell onto his friend, who had been sleeping through the whole affair under his tent.

---

151. I was so pissed because it was a hike every night to store all our food into bear boxes and these rednecks left all their stuff strewn about. The rest of it was stupid human tricks but I remember thinking it was too bad a bear hadn't shown up to eat another bad folksinger.

It surprised every man and beast when he rose up and staggered out from the heap of material, moaning because his friend had just stepped on him. We'd had no idea he was under there.

The elk did not like this new development one bit.

"Get back," I instructed Wolfgang and Beth.[152] They beat a quick retreat. We watched from the relative safety of our camps as the rednecks, one dressed only in untied hiking books and his underwear, scrambled away with their lives. Before the herd of elk ran off in the other direction, they trampled over coolers and kicked down the remaining tent. As the animals tore across the open field, I noted a thick quilt waving from one male's antlers.

The ranger refunded our camp fees and let us know that those boys would not be returning. They were squatters to begin with, but during the high season he said park staff could only keep up with so much. Later, pedaling out of Jasper, we saw two guys walking along the side of the road, one with a guitar that looked familiar to us strapped to his back.

They waved and hooted when they saw our mule train, as if nothing untoward had occurred just hours before.

Enzo waved back.

"There's a couple of guys who know how to make the past the past," Beth said.

152. All I remember is that Joe was packing us up and he would get so focused when he got us ready to ship out. It was a secret Joe method, this packing; it changed slightly every day so there was no way for anyone but Joe to pack our gear. Incidentally, this freed him from breakfast prep and morning child care duties. He may have yelled something as we fought the rednecks fighting the elk, but we were already washing our hands of the whole thing. The elk seemed plenty capable of fending for themselves at that point. I do remember Joe going to get the ranger at that point . . . again. The boys were sitting on a picnic table laughing hysterically. They looked like fans at a baseball game.

Chapter 28

Gone to the Dogs

I'm gonna . . . I'm gonna break my rusty cage and run.
—Johnny Cash (lyrics by Chris Cornell)

The thrill was gone. Not that I exactly relished being ambushed by roadside mutts, having to outpedal packs of pit bulls hunting my rear wheel like wolves on the tundra, or best the snarling junkyard German shepherd homing in on my spinning calves as if they were drumsticks, but there is something to be said for the thrill of the chase.

Panic, adrenaline, flight, that brief window when you don't know if you'll outrun chomping canines until a final kick of speed and a few braveheart howls gets you over. Few activities shock the monkey like a

good sprint to safety . . . or allow you to live more fully in the present.

Tag. It's one of the first games children learn.

Only the dogs along Canada's highways and byways had stopped playing with us.

We'd see them pop up and take their position as always, but when they got a better look at the mule train, its length, girth, and how many souls we were bringing to bear down on them, dogs of every stripe turned tail and ran, or dropped down on their haunches, making themselves small and inconspicuous.

The first few times this made me laugh and filled me with a predatory power. I watched a few mutts back into their driveways. "Spread the word, pooch, there's a new sheriff in town."

But as it turned out, it's lonely at the top. No one plays with the lion and his cubs.

Dogs weren't alone in this new order of things. We parted most of the animal population of western Canada in our wake. Big-horned sheep, cougars, horses, elk, deer—the day we spooked a big black bear enjoying some roadside berries, I felt invincible. Every last animal had the same *what in hell?* expression, followed by sheer panic as we'd chug past. Only the moose wasn't impressed, but that discovery was still hundreds of miles away.

While we were untouchable, Beth and her single touring bike . . . not so much. She'd made nervous jokes about cougars all the way up the northern run of Vancouver Island.

"Remember how Steve said they'll snatch a child in a flash and leave nothing but a business card?"

The problem was, after the hills of Salt Spring Island incident, we

couldn't trust a word out our city-dwelling friend's mouth, no matter how much conviction he'd put into the warning.

Sitting in my rearview mirror, sometimes twenty-five yards back, more often a quarter mile or more off the pace, Beth lived in a state of readiness reserved for bomb silo minutemen.

She wheeled up as I was taking a photo of another road sign that had caught my eye.

DO NOT FEED BEARS

$50,000 FINE WILDLIFE ACT

"Not that anyone cares about my safety, but that sounds like you'll second-mortgage the house if they eat me right off the bike. 'Cause technically, you'll be feeding the bears."

I laughed. But she was only half joking. Without my knowledge, she'd learned how to use her voice, a bike pump, and the heel of her shoes to command respect from a number of dogs. Beth's a realist; she was steeling herself to battle with bigger creatures.[153]

After another chase we knew nothing about, Beth had had enough. We'd regrouped at the top of a hill.

"Not that anyone cares about my safety," she repeated. "But when you come upon a pack of dogs, or whatnot, looking for a fight, if you have any love in your hearts for the woman who gave you life, and yes that includes you old man, 'cause you'd be a zombie without me, stop and protect my honor . . . and body parts. That's all I ask."

Truth was, we hadn't even noticed the last pack of dogs.

---

153. I felt an acute sense of solitude. I never felt so alone as when dogs would sprint out of their driveways bearing down on me while I tried to go up hills—not very fast. The whole time I cursed my husband and children's names for leaving me alone to fend for myself.

"I did," Enzo volunteered.

Beth gave me "the look."

I shrugged, innocence incarnate.

Cute and cuddly boys. Cute and cuddly. Maybe she'll take pity on our general obliviousness and testosterone poisoning.

"You look like you survived all right, Mom," Quinn noted.

What my boys still had to learn about women. Just stop talking, gents. I removed my helmet in a show of respect.

"I promise to keep a weather eye out for animals of any size. And you have our word—right, boys?—that we'll wait until you've passed without incident before we ride on. Nothing's gonna chase you again without backup."

The boys nodded. Whatever Dad said. Beth didn't look entirely sold but what could she say in the face of such compliance.

"We'll see."

We pedaled on.

True to our word, the next time we happened upon dogs, I brought the train to a halt. We waited for Beth to roll through. As she arrived Quinn and Enzo hollered and gestured at the befuddled animals, waving lightsabers in an exaggerated show of chivalry.

"Very funny," she said.

So it happened to be a group of wiener dogs waiting across the blacktop from us. We weren't taking any chances. One gave up a little chirp of a bark as Beth came close, but the other two dogs seemed to sense their predicament and promptly chased him off.

As we pedaled beside Beth for a bit, she turned and offered a smile of real gratitude.

"I know you think that was just a joke, but it felt good, you guys having my back like that. Even if it was for dogs the size of my big toe this time."

I gave her my best *knight at your service, me lady* nod.

"It's the principle of it, you know?" Beth said.

"Honey, we won't hang you out there again . . . unless we don't see it coming."

Her smile dimmed a little.

"Always giving yourself an out . . ."

And that boys, is why you quit at the nod.

We'd been trained to expect all wildlife, at least roadside wildlife, to step back if not run away from the mule train, at worst to ignore our presence on that beast of a bike contraption. I had excellent photos of the backsides of animals in motion to prove it.

Only the moose didn't get the memo. We would learn too late that grizzly bears fear moose, so by default we would have done well to fear

them. And we did, keeping a safe distance from the one standing off the road in the tall brush, but we had too much faith in the prowess of the mule train.

"Let me dig out my camera."

"Dad!"

I didn't have to hear anything else. The tone in his voice said it all. I started pedaling without a look over my shoulder. I'd heard hooves and snorts and that was enough for me. My quick reactions probably gave us the edge. It gave me hope, anyway.

I can't say how long we pedaled, but in a twisted way it felt good to be the prey again, to run for our lives. The life-or-death sprint definitely blew out the king-of-the-jungle cobwebs and put us back where we belonged, at the edge of our seats and our abilities. I looked back long enough to see that my crew was still on board.

"What's the moose doing now, boys?"

"Dad," Quinn said. He was my eyes. I waited for the status report. "I think we just left Mom by herself to deal with a moose."

"It's not chasing us?"

"Not anymore."

"Oh crap." I turned the big rig around, using both sides of the highway to execute a wide circle. We kept up a good head of steam back into the thick of it. If we hadn't alerted the moose the first time through with our yacht-sized rig, Beth wouldn't be a sitting duck. We'd gotten the animal good and mad, then left town.

"You see it?" I kept yelling. The boys yelling back "No" or "Nothing yet." We needed a hyperspace button or gear or something. I dug deep for a bit more torque, not wanting to let Beth down after giving our word for the hundredth time. I looked at the canister of bear spray strapped to my handlebar, trying to remember if the fine print indicated it having any effect on moose.

That's when we blew right by her. The boys called out to their mother as we whistled past. Little Matteo laughed. I looked up from my bear spray bottle.

Another wide circle and we were beside her.

"We came to rescue you from the moose," Quinn said.

"It chased us," Enzo added.

"You mean that moose?"

We'd made it almost all the way back to where the great nonchase had begun. Only the moose was twenty-five yards farther off the highway munching brush close to where we'd left him.

"Careful now," I said.

"Dad." Enzo this time. "I never actually saw the moose come after us."

Beth smiled. "If it means anything, I had a ringside view and I never saw anything chasing you. But I watched the mule train of fools

take off like it was the end of the world." She rolled over to give each of us a kiss. "Either way, I love you guys for coming back."

The moose didn't look out of breath.

As I caught mine, I kept the big animal in my sights. I just don't trust 'em. It's a safe bet they feel the same way about us.

Either way, it was good to know we could still run for our lives.

Chapter 29

Trucker's Dream

After months of want and hunger, we suddenly found ourselves able to have meals fit for the gods, and with appetites the gods might have envied.
—Ernest Shackleton

A rain that came up fast and late in the day's ride chased us inside. I blinked away the last of it—cold, fat raindrops that make you stamp and shiver—so I could take in the truck stop menu.

Beth eyed the flophouse motel on the other side of the window.

Even though it was Canada, I scanned the parking lot for packs of stray dogs and prostitutes. I came up empty but for a man by a motel door blowing smoke rings into the downpour. A bar advertising dancers and "top shelf" liquor separated the two establishments.

"Is this a dump?" asked Quinn. Somehow during our trip, he'd gotten onto a part-time quest to understand the hierarchy of hotels and motels we passed. He'd point to a roadside motel and ask me where it fell on the scale. A true "dump" had not been checked off his list.

"There are different shades of dumps," Beth offered in a bid for a teachable moment, a chance to instill our son with the wisdom that outward appearance might not so easily define inner character. That's when the waitress mentioned that if we wanted a room we'd need to see the bartender next door.

"It's a dump," I said. "But it's the only port in the storm."

We'd tried several other ports earlier in the day. A campground touting a swimming pool and putt-putt golf had been closed for renovations, and a provincial park by a lake was shut tight thanks to the twin infestations of grizzly bears and mosquitoes. We'd have been willing to brave the bears.

"Order me whatever you're having." With that Beth excused herself to the bathroom. I imagined cracked mirrors and broken toiletry vending machines. Beth was hoping more for a hand dryer than a mirror.

In once festive colors across a grease stained marquee above the open kitchen I saw all the menu I needed:

TRUCKER'S DREAM

PRIZES AWARDED IF FINISHED IN ONE SITTING

The waitress was not in the habit of asking people to repeat their orders. She merely leaned on her hip and waited for me to correct myself.

I reordered mac-and-cheese for my boys and said, "And two Trucker's Dreams."

She delivered an unsympathetic smile. "You might want to think about this, Chief. No one's ever eaten two dreams at once."

Beth slipped back into the booth at that moment and I said, "The other one's for her."

Miners and roughneck oil workers in stained long coats crowding adjacent booths took a closer look at us.

I pointed at our bikes parked outside, to explain our appetites. But every man was looking at my wife. A woman who can eat her weight in hash is a keeper in the North Country. You could read their skepticism, though: By then Beth had lost the last of the weight she'd gained with Matteo. Hour upon hour in the saddle during our trip had carved her into performance art. She resembled an Olympic swimmer with a boob job. If Beth ate the Trucker's Dream I might have to fight our way out of there to keep her, but she would enter into undying legend in these parts.

Without knowing what was in the actual dish, the outcome was never in doubt. A cyclist pulling a single rig with panniers eats like a termite. One hauling fifteen feet of bike train, three children, and hundreds of pounds of gear along the Yellowhead Highway knows no mortal bounds.

When the dreams arrived at our table I decided that God did exist, if only inside that greasy spoon.

Three thick slabs of meat—roast beef, Salisbury steak maybe, and something else unidentifiable—formed the foundation of the Trucker's Dream. It was a hell of a platform on which to build a masterpiece. Gravy formed an adhesive layer between each course. Sitting atop the meat slabs were three over-easy eggs, gravy, three cuts of breakfast ham, gravy, three massive dollops of mashed potatoes, each with its own pool of butter, but—in a delicate artistic decision—no gravy this time. Instead cheese formed adhesive. And that's when the creators of this dream went off the map and into my heart. It's as if it dawned on them that there might be a health nut at the table. In the same dollop shape as the potatoes, we were treated to scoops of canned veggies. If they'd stopped there, I'd have been impressed. Instead, those crazy bastards behind the grill went for broke. Gravy secured a hamburger to the center of veggie mountain, and lettuce, tomato, and pickles reached for the heavens. Atop whitecapped peaks of mashed potatoes stood toothpick flags of the Canadian Maple Leaf and Old Glory. A moment of silence, please, while a choir of schoolchildren sing both national anthems.

The waitress reached in, lit the whole damn thing on fire, and called it good.

She didn't, actually. But the room was a powder keg of expectations. In the fixed full view of the big dull eyes of men who often forget to take off their work gloves while they eat, I winked at my wife and—so in love with life and each other at that moment—we went to town on those entrées.

There was no sharing any of it with the children, no talk of the meal's magnitude, no grim determination to soldier on or rationalizing why we couldn't finish this or that part of the dream. We savored it all,

toasted our fortunes, and handed out toothpick flags to the children when that was all that was left on our plates.

Then, in an act that should not be misconstrued as smug, over-the-top American bragging, I ordered apple pie à la mode for the entire table.

In truth, this was to avoid the inevitable nighttime wake-up call. I'm consumed by hunger to the point that I feel stomach acids churning around like mercenaries searching for something to destroy. That pie was a basic survival.

When our waitress cleared the dream plates she held them high and did a little ballerina turn for the room. Applause, hoots, and a rumble of satisfied grunts filled the restaurant.

We'd crossed the Rubicon.

"I kinda like this dump," Quinn said.

When the prizes arrived Beth had her back turned, studying some murals painted on long saws and rotary blades. There's something about pastoral scenes lovingly detailed on heavy industrial equipment that makes it hard to look away.

The prizes took my breath away. Truly. Nothing could have been more inappropriately appropriate than what I'd been handed.

"Absolutely not," Beth said.

"Let me see," said Enzo.

I held the two pristine mud flaps featuring silver silhouettes of naked ladies at bay.

"Come on, honey, they're folkloric, culturally significant markers in our lives."

She rolled her eyes.

"We could secure them to the bikes as extra fender protection against Portland's wet winters."

"They're not coming with us," she said. "Unless we're planning to ride to divorce court."

Beth does not suffer foolish husbands who make their wives NFL season widows, or park themselves at the bars instead of coming home to bathe their boys, fix them dinner, and make up knuckle-biting adventure stories before bed.

I wouldn't want her any other way. Even when I want it other ways. Which is why I shipped those coveted mud flaps to my friend in Arizona—for safekeeping until such time as Beth says they can come home.

A bachelor, he has secured them to his commuter bike and rolls, in all his ridiculous, Easy Rider glory, around the bone-dry desert. And a bachelor, I trust, he will stay.

Chapter 30

Hailstorms Are All We Know of Heaven[154]

I believe in God, only I spell it Nature.

—Frank Lloyd Wright

The heavens opened up and started throwing hail balls the size of buck-eyes when we were within spitting distance of the home of some friends. New friends, as it happened, that we'd made on Salt Spring Island. They'd

---

154. When the hail began to rain down in earnest, and the novelty of it wore off—I realized I'd given away my gloves to Enzo, and my socks to Quinn, while my rain-coat and pants were in Joe's pannier a quarter mile ahead of me. I basically took on an angry god throwing fastballs while dressed in sporty summer wear. My defense: It had been summer ten minutes before. That's Canada, folks.

told us to look them up when we got to Edmonton.

Fair warning: Don't wave a welcome sign around us Kurmaskies unless you mean it. We'll take you up on even the most casual mention of hospitality. And if you're foolish enough to hand over a business card or scribble a phone number on a scrap of paper—we understand how you were swept up in the moment and momentum and boisterous carnival that is our family—expect us on your doorstep.

We had maybe a five-minute warning before all hell broke loose. So close—only five kilometers left to go after more than a hundred care-free kilometers we'd rolled already. And much of it had been down-right hot. Warmth and sunshine has a way of creating a certain amount of giddy, if unrealistic optimism. I thought we could outrun that angry squall line or duck under an overpass if it caught us.

When the skies opened, it seemed fun at first. But what began as laughter over the oddity that was ice shavings the size of fingernails dancing off our forearms and melting on our gloves turned to panic when the hail swelled to the size of peanut M&M's, something sent straight from the Old Testament, hurling down.

A minute or two of this pounding and the boys were done. But there was nowhere to go. It was just highway and hail, highway and hail. Highway to hail. An AC/DC song popped into my head. I looked around, holding my arm over my eyes to block the hail long enough to see for more than five feet. Sometimes the only way to get through is to go through. The boys started to whimper, and I started to lose it. Doing my best to comfort them, I think I actually said something about this being a big adventure, right before I pulled into a ditch so I could use my body to shield them. Then through the deluge I thought

I spotted something—a steeple perhaps?

Jesus Saves! after all.

What should have been a turnoff ramp came up short. It was exactly like riding to the edge of a cartoon that's still being drawn. The subdivision, thrown together in record time by the looks of it, was still being born. A steep, sloshy dip stood between us and a sprint on pavement through the parking lot to the church. I got the boys off the bike and told them to run for a door. I prayed for an awning or an overhang. I'd be right behind them.

When they couldn't find enough purchase to clear the backside of the ravine, I clamored down and pushed them up through the muck, one by one. Back at the bike, a quick peek found Matteo safe and dry and chuckling in the trailer. I kept talking to him so he wouldn't start crying, or maybe so I wouldn't.

I saw my boys reach the church before I gripped our bike contraption as best I could and entered the short, muddy ravine—sliding down with any sort of control was similar to wrestling a steer to the ground. But that was no more than a warm-up. Getting hundreds of pounds of bike and gear up a muddy hill in a hailstorm in clip-in sandals . . . ridiculously hard. I made it halfway up the slope before I found myself running in place, unable to get enough purchase and about to slide back. In a move of primal desperation, I turned those sandals into makeshift crampons, jamming them into the soft mud. It worked. I laughed out loud.

That day's ride had gone from fun, to funny, to bad, to panic, to oh come on!, to funny again. What else can one do in that situation? With each sandal jab into the loose, wet slope, I hollered to give my-

self strength, issuing the laughter of a madman in between.

When I had to hold the entire mule train in place just below the top of the hill to suck in a breath and reposition my grip, I yelled out, "I've wanted to try cyclocross, but not today!"

It's not a healthy place to find oneself, talking out loud when no one's around. But it helped.

After summiting, I realized that someone had to let Beth know we'd turned off, abandoned ship/highway, what have you. This required going down and up the ravine again, much easier this time without the bike. And my crampon skills were improving. I stepped onto the shoulder of the road and waved a pair of safety vests above my head, air-craft-carrier-flag-man-style, and hoped she saw me. I continued to wave the vests as I ran for the church, just to give her a fighting chance. I imagine I resembled a large flightless bird in full retreat.[155]

Then it was down and up, grab the bike, and break into a sprint for the boys, church, and what I hoped was relative safety.

Beth saw my flag demonstration, somehow. We would laugh about all of this someday. She managed to find us huddling under the church entrance, baby asleep in the warm, dry trailer. The church was still under construction—doors locked, parking lot empty.

Apparently, Jesus wanted us to help ourselves from there on.

We were freezing now that we'd stopped moving. It was time to get my people out of wet clothes and into sleeping bags. As much as I wanted to curl us together in a pile of sleeping bags and call it a night, it was 4 PM.

---

155. He resembled a big muddy white man doing avant garde theater while being chased by bees. But I did see him.

I thought of our dear friends, the ones we'd met once at an outdoor café for half an hour, sharing laughs, a picnic table, and extra fries together. They'd have been heartbroken if we'd stood them (and their warm beds, barbecue, and playmates for the boys) up.

I wiggled out of my bag. It felt like leaving a tent on Everest. I took Beth's bike—she gave me her blessing by way of a quick nod before she burrowed back into the bag to nurse Matteo—out to the road behind the church. The hail had stopped, but lightning was there to fill the void.

Navigating a semi-built subdivision, designed as if the car would rule the world forever, was no fun. A painter's van nearly sideswiped me. Then I had to backtrack out of two cul-de-sacs before I managed to find a Husky gas station, call our friends, and put a rescue in the wind.

A few hours later we were eating ribs in the warmth of Corine and Kevin's home; laughing, hearing stories about the time Corine called Mother Teresa's direct phone number (and she answered), listening to Michael Franti, and learning how to survive a day at the world's largest mall.

Life turns like that. The trick is staying limber enough to turn with it, and a pair of sandal crampons never hurts.

Chapter 31

I Will Miss This Body So Much When It's Gone

There is still no cure for the common birthday.
—John Glenn

I caught my reflection in a mirror. Beth let me shower first on account of how simultaneously cold and sweaty I was at the end of a hundred kilometers.

We'd spent long, satisfying days pedaling a windblown road between Edmonton and Saskatoon. Somewhere along the way my body began to react in a different way than earlier in the trip. The harder the riding, the more strength I came back with the next day. When I'd dis-

mount in the evenings, I'd kinda glow and shake and feel a hum in my bones. No longer on the verge of folding or about to crumble anymore. Hitting on all cylinders, some people call it. Another level. Somewhere I'd never been before. Could this be what elite racers felt?

I started to towel off, then stopped. I hadn't seen my body naked in ages.

Jesus.

It stunned me.

I was going to miss this body so much when it was gone . . . To own one of these, carved and trimmed, skin pressed against muscles and veins. To own it even for a little while was the most dangerous of propositions. A pitch-perfect machine that when pushed and pulled, when let out to run wide open, will perform complicated acts of skill and daring with an easy grace.

Realizing I was in possession of such a prize, it made me a little punch-drunk. Now flexing it here and bending it there. Why not? I counted five or six separate striations dividing the sections of my calves. I had veins in places I'd never seen before, worming across my chest even. Someone had jammed baseballs under the skin of my upper arms.

I didn't notice Beth until she was behind me in the mirror. Usually, she would have given me grief for anything smacking of narcissism, but this time she hugged me from behind.

"I wasn't navel gazing, baby. Well, I was a little, but look at me."

I struck a crab pose.

"I've never seen you in better shape," she agreed. "Out of hand, but in a good way."

I picked up my towel. "It's both beautiful and sad, you know. I

think this is it. I'll never look or feel better than I do right now."

Beth smacked my rear pretty hard. "You Irishmen and your tragic edges." She turned me around and gave me a tender kiss. "You're forty-two years old and still able to drag most of a zip code behind you on a bicycle . . . and get to look like this for a while in the bargain."

She was talking about gratitude. I peered into the mirror one more time. I felt it.

"Would you take a picture of me?" I asked.

"Would you get the hell out of here?" Smiling, letting me know she understood, but let's not get carried away with ourselves. "And watch the boys. There's no cartoon channel so God knows what they've settled on out there."

She threw me a pose of her own. I couldn't believe how much her body had changed in a few short months. Then the door slammed in my face.

This is how it works: You ride until you don't. The rest is just excuses, waiting, and stuff done to survive. We get these machines of flesh and bone for only a while—that will one day fail us utterly. In the meantime, if you connect yours to a bicycle it might bring you to stand one day in front of a mirror, staring at legs like iron rods and bones that hum the body electric. That reflection will knock you back, so beautiful and so fleeting you'll want to weep, even if you aren't Irish.

Whether you hammer at thirty miles an hour with sponsors written on your back, or it's your first go and you top out at ten mph with no one watching. Just go . . . so you'll have a body worth missing when it's gone.

PART FIVE

Nova Scotia

Mom

We press a button for the third floor. If it were up to me, Mom would be living in my home. Instead the elevator deposits us in Paris. Each floor of her retirement village is themed after a country. We're greeted by a colossal image of the Eiffel Tower. My guess is the selection process weighed heavily in favor of travel atlas wallpapers that were on sale.

Mom thinks it's fate. At least she does today. Her thoughts are still fluid but scatter like autumn leaves some days.

"I speak French. You know I went to school in San Moritz?" There it is again. Talking to me like we've only met recently.

"I was meant to live on this floor."

We pass a man in a Mickey Mouse T-shirt, slacks pulled up to just below his nipples and a pair of California Casuals that he thinks pass for shoes but everyone else can see are slippers. I imagine Frenchmen beating him senseless with day-old baguettes before banishing him back to Miami Beach.

"The fourth floor is Florida," Mom says.

Meaning Slipperman won't have far to go.

"I would have been okay with that, I guess."

We moved to the real Florida when I was ten. Every time I visit the retirement village, Mom asks outright why she's not still there. Or she waxes passive-aggressively nostalgic for the sun, the warmth, the hot tubs she never went in, or the company of my youngest brother, who had to choose between his marriage and keeping Mom in Florida near him.

"Why would a woman with severe rheumatoid arthritis move to the

287

damp . . . dampness of Portland, Oregon?"

She knows the answer to this even on her most scattered days. Starting with the fall that nearly ended her, the screws in her arms, the crushing depression over my father's death, the dehydration, and missed meds, culminating in a family conference call.

Only in America do we put our parents out to pasture by boxing them up with a couple hundred other bridge-playing peers. I lobbied hard to have her move in with me. I was overruled, for what my family thinks is for my own good.

Perhaps, but I leave bits of my heart like bread crumbs every time I walk beside the Seine River wallpaper to her room.

Mom never learned how to play bridge.

Even though the place is pretty decent as far are these places go, it's not . . . right.

Their slogan is "Five Star Retirement Living." To which, Mom, showing that she still has her humor intact, is pleased to inform anyone that "one of the stars seems to have gone missing."

We walk slowly along. Arm in arm, for support and affection. She has a cane that she despises but does use.

"Thank God I don't live on the fifth floor." Here it comes. She offers up the next bit in a stage whisper. "China."

Forget for a moment that most of her apartment is crowded with antiques from the Orient, scrolls from teahouses, pottery from Okanagwa— places where her own mother worked as a professor and she frequently visited. My childhood was a tapestry of incredible stories from around the globe, told by an openhearted woman who closed out her own teaching career instructing homebound children—sick, blind, deformed, dying.

In our home we were asked to consider not the shell of a person but what it held as precious.

I want to believe these episodes of inadvertent racism—one or two per visit—are sponsored by the pharmaceutical industry and the ravages of time. Or maybe it has to do with a steady diet of the Fox News Network shouting hate and fear . . . and bite-sized morsels of Hollywood gossip at the top and bottom of every hour. Countless couch-bound retirees defenseless to the onslaught. I hear it hollering out from under the doorjambs as I walk the halls. A chilling blanket of self-righteous certainty seeping into everything. In the dining room of her village I hear guys in the buffet line channeling Bill O'Reilly word for word. Or do we all start to close up as we get older?

"I don't know what it is . . . but I wouldn't want to live up there." She uses her cane to point up.

In these moments I resort to humor, a shared language we've communicated in our whole lives. "But just think how much faster your laundry would get done up there. All the live chickens running the halls might be a hazard, but you'd have your cane to swat at them."

Her smile surfaces. "Oh Joe. You're making fun of me now." My mother's laughter remains one of my first memories. It's something I will always need more of.

"Yes. I am." Playfully nudging her as much as a six-foot-two, two-hundred-pound man dares nudge a seventy-year-old lady with bones of balsawood.

Teasing was cherished in our house as long as it came clever and illuminating. Bring your best Dorothy Parker or your wittiest Oscar Wilde or stay home. Clumsy insults and brutish name calling was an embarrass-

ment brought upon yourself.

"Do you have to go, already?"

I smile in the doorway. The Arc de Triomphe covered the entire wall behind me, acting as a halo.

"We'll always have Paris," I say, spreading my arms wide as if effortlessly holding up the famous archway.

I wait a moment longer at the closed door. Her laughter muffled now but still there, then drowned out completely by the sound of a television.

Chapter 32

Performance Art

The purpose of art is washing the dust of daily life off our souls.
—Pablo Picasso

The wind kicking off the Bay of Fundy was all wrong for a full day of loaded bicycle touring, but we didn't care. After a summer in the saddles rolling the far reaches of Canada, we were still raring to go.

A happy surprise each day we saddled up.

Nova Scotia's bracing sea air, hand-crank ferry rides, whitewashed churches, empty back roads, and explosions of autumn colors had much to do with this, though it's not an overstatement to say my family had found its true rhythm. The change of seasons was something we

couldn't deny anymore. It's what would send us home shortly, not our physical or emotional failings. That was a point of pride with me.

While we hadn't pedaled the length of Canada—only four thousand or so miles of it—measuring a family adventure in any terms other than good times spent in the company of the ones you love, learning what they're capable of and who they can become on and off the bikes, would be bad math.

Cape Breton is the edge of the world. And the Cabot Trail is one of North America's premier adventures on the edge of that edge. Riding it during those final days of our tour, what struck me was how tame it felt to us. I'm not saying it is, I'm just conveying how we perceived it. After the Yellowhead, everything felt smaller. The leaves were a bonfire of reds, yellows, and burnt oranges. We could see across the width of the island a hundred times a day and watch the workings of man in the little villages below. We took advantage of the scale of things and our level of fitness to stop even more than usual, playing games of tag, gathering leaves and buckeyes near waterfalls, lingering at vista points. Sitting together sometimes we'd recount moments of the trip; more often we'd stare out at the ocean and enjoy comfortable silences with one another.

Danny was about to shove off on a fully loaded bicycle into a thrashing of weather, but we convinced him to stay inside the Tim Hortons a little longer, to tell us his story.

Beth had become quite a regular of Tim Hortons, which is Canada's answer to Dunkin' Donuts with a better color scheme and what Beth told me was a higher grade of coffee beans. The boys encouraged these stops not out of any concern for Beth's addiction, but

as part of a continuing campaign to see how many doughnuts they could talk us out of.

Danny looked like the son of an Ivy League professor.

"My ride is a performance art project."

Aren't they all.

"No, I mean I got a grant to pedal around Canada, set up inside galleries, art museums, and places you wouldn't expect like coffee-houses, outside fire stations, and in department store windows."

He had our attention.

"I set up a bike tree repair stand and go to work. Sometimes the sponsoring location has spread the word so there are already bikes for me to work on, other times I work on my own bike and people ask what I'm doing. Pretty soon some of them bring in their bikes for repairs. I teach them how to repair it right there in the gallery or grocery store, so it's interactive."

Quinn nodded. "Do you do paintings of the bikes?"

"No," Danny said. "It's not that kind of art. The act of doing this on a time-based basis, in places you wouldn't normally find it. That's the statement."

I thought of the postmodern exhibits I'd toured throughout my life. Some of the best parts of a bike tour are all the museums you get to stop in. I once walked behind a group who were viewing dots on walls, shrink-wrapped bloody mannequins, and river stones arranged around the plastic head of a toy chicken. Their teacher was going on and on about the significance of this and that. He sounded smarter than I could ever hope to be. When the group stopped in front of the next piece, he launched into a lengthy speech about the overpowering need to be in control and the security blankets we cover ourselves in, but in reality there is no such thing as safety, just degrees of risk. Then he came closer to see what number it was in the catalog. That's when the security guard leaned over and said, not unkindly, "Sir, that would be our fire extinguisher."

In that light, Danny's project was a masterpiece. Not only did it give people something to talk about, but Danny's performance art changed the world around him, touched lives, and had a utilitarian purpose. Let a shrink-wrapped mannequin try that.

"My dad thinks it's an excuse to put off law school for another year and ride my bike around Canada."

We stood beside our bikes under the awning of Tim Hortons waiting for the weather to break.

"Is it?" I asked.

"Of course," Danny said. "But does that make the project any less

valid?"

I thought about what I was doing for a living, riding my family across Canada, then writing about it. Reaching out through words, maybe influencing someone to take up the bike, break out of the matrix, and set off on their own adventure. Maybe not.

At least Danny could point at some tangible results when he rolled out of a town. He could see them rolling away from him.

I nodded my approval, then reached out and gave Danny a Roman handshake, the one where you grip each other's forearms. He liked that.

I excused myself to the bathroom. When I came back, Danny and his overloaded mobile repair shop on two wheels had pushed off into the angry afternoon. Beth was sitting on the bench under a stand-up patio heater sipping coffee and looking me over. I thought it was for stray toilet paper that was stuck to my shoes again, or because I'd changed out of a sweaty jersey and into a less sweaty one.

"Danny said to tell you he knew who you were."

I looked at her. That sounded a bit outlaw. Like we were on the run and Danny was a bounty hunter.

"He just wanted you to know that *Metal Cowboy* had a big influence on him. And it played a part when he decided to meld bike touring with his art project idea."

I was grinning now from ear to ear.

"See . . . I wasn't gonna tell you," Beth said. "'Cause you get enough gratification from your writing and props from people and, you know, you're already excitable."

True.

"There's more," Beth said. "He thinks you come across like the guy

in your books." Smiling, she added, "So you've fooled another one."

Most of the time we don't find out whether our actions, the things we do and say, have any effect on the world. I could lie and say I write it down for noble reasons, but the consuming truth is that I'd be swallowed whole if I didn't. It's that simple.

It's the same reason I ride.

Chapter 33

It's for You

A man, as a general rule, owes very little to what he is born with—a man is what he makes of himself.

—Alexander Graham Bell

Alexander Graham Bell chose Cape Breton to escape civilization so he could conjure up some rather useful tools for it. Tools that have brought us together and, recently, to my way of thinking, become toys too much of the time, ones that put distance between people standing right next to each other, not to mention cause some horrific car accidents.

While he invented the telephone he kept everyone he cared about close enough to talk to them in person. He moved his family to Cape Breton so his children run wild and free of the constraints of society where, as he put it, they could wear jeans. I wonder what Bell would have thought of social media. I know where I stand. The final post on my Facebook page, before I stopped checking it, says it all:

> What's on your mind?
>   Tweet you. An unscientific survey by me concludes that 98 percent of Tweets and Facebook entries, including this one, are the social media equivalent of Tourette's syndrome: explosions of nonsensical babble that go like this: "I like puppies!" (I don't care.) "Bought too much mayo at Sam's Club, want some?" (Sure, wait, you live in Florida, you numbskull. I'm four thousand miles from that mayo.) "My mood is fierce and I'm ready for action!" (Your mood is desperate and you're ready for bed so stop typing inane comments.) All day long, it goes like this, around and around the world. Technology has inadvertently created the most powerful

communication tool in the universe and we've turned it into a perpetual verbal diarrhea machine. I'm not saying I don't want to hear from you, my friend. But let's cut out the middleman. Why not save something for when we get together? Or call me when you have something to say. A funny story, or when you need a ride, wanna take a ride, or grab a bite, or if you've found a bag of money that you want to share. If you gotta share everything, make it witty, have a point, use phrases other than *My bad*, *It's all good*, or *ROFL* when it wasn't even LOL. I don't want to know if you feel a coffee break coming on, crave chicken Marsala for dinner, or wonder if you have a drinking problem. On that last one, if you put that on Facebook, the answer is yes. Bring your most acerbic tongue or your drollest humor to the keyboard, or sit on your hands, tape those idle fingers together if you have to, until you can think of something to say. In the first year Xerox introduced the copier, over half of all printing was of employees' private parts. It improved only slightly over time. An even bleaker future awaits social media if we keep sucking away one another's precious time with these involuntary spasms. So if you need me, you can't Tweet me. I'll be holed up in a small Montana cabin, finishing my manifesto. Come in person. That way we can see each other when we talk about a way out of this mess.

We didn't take a cell phone on the Canada bike ride and against all odds and fears from friends and family, we survived. When we crossed into Canada, it went into the glove box of the car without ceremony.

If you're counting on GPS, cell coverage, and the like to save you, you're betting on the wrong horse. It might, but to substitute it for resourcefulness, good decision making, and survival skills is foolhardy.

For fun, we'd ask people in the parks and campgrounds how their coverage was. Sometimes they'd shake their heads and frown.

But the real reason I left that phone back at Steve and Mel's is that it's an intrusion on the experience of living: mine, yours, theirs. In Jasper we were standing on the shore of a remote island. It had taken an hour by boat to get there. Standing at the base of a glacier with my

family, marveling at the translucent blue ice, a cell phone rang a few feet behind us. We flinched.

"Nothing. Just standing here looking at some blue ice."

It would have been so easy to snatch the device from his mitt and chuck it into deep water before he knew what had happened.

I controlled myself . . . and for that there will always be a clot of regret lodged in my bloodstream.

Our day at the Alexander Graham Bell Museum was more tranquil. A sign at the gate informed tourists to shut off all cell phones and electronic devices before entering.

Bell wanted the world to connect, but after spending a few hours in the echo chamber of his presence, I'm certain he never meant for it to intrude, or take the place of living.

Chapter 34

The Victory Tuck

A tough push through a day of pounding rainstorms to reach our destination, but now that we're here, all is forgiven. I'm set to perform at The Lobster Galley, sharing the bill with someone named Buddy McCallister.

To the backbeat of more rain hammering the roof of a harborside dinner club, we cut loose for an evening of stories and live Celtic music. Buddy turned out to be a Grammy-winning legend, but you wouldn't have known it from the way he treated people, the way he shared the stage with all the local musicians backing him. Pennywhistles, powerful fits of drumming, a cappella voices, harmonizing choruses, soaring ballads that tapped into something deep within my Irish DNA. Before the entrées arrived, I was humbled to be sharing the spotlight with Buddy and his crew. When Quinn mustered the courage to ask how one plays the spoons, Buddy came down from the stage, with great effort, since he walked with difficulty, to offer a tutorial, before he handed over the spoons.

"You can keep those," he said.

Frayed tape and scuffed edges; those spoons hadn't come from the galley kitchen. Like us, they'd traveled a great distance to make a few hours of joyful noise together. The evening ended with encores, stories,

and a glorious step-dancing mosh pit finale. Quinn slept with Buddy's spoons grasped tightly for the rest of the trip and plays them to this day.

On that evening, mind you, we did not know Buddy's standing in the music community. We knew his standing in our eyes, but it wasn't until we were back home listening to *Thistle and Shamrock* on NPR one Saturday evening, that we heard Fiona Ritchie introduce Buddy as the Grammy-winning legend. He started to play and we connected the dots.

Quinn got down his spoons from the place of honor over the sink where we kept them and jammed around the kitchen to with the radio-waved version of his friend Buddy.

We pull over at Pirate's Cove for lunch and some swordplay. It's perhaps a day's pedal to Halifax, where a plane will wing us home. Beth's mother is dying. Her second mother to die in one lifetime. Nancy married Beth's father when Beth was two, and while she carried the title of stepmom, it was purely semantics; Beth was losing a mother, again. We dangle our feet in the water while the boys skip stones. Thirteen is the record so far. What waits for us back home no amount of pedaling can fix.

"Remember when we only owned enough stuff so that we were one yard sale from the road at all times?" Beth says. "This summer made me feel like that again."

It's Beth's way of telling me that she's had the time of her life.

Our Trucker's Dream prizes are stowed deep in the panniers: those two pristine mud flaps featuring silver silhouettes of naked ladies.

I lobby my case one more time. I lose my case again.

When I go into the post office to ship some things home, I'm asked to show the contents of the box before I seal it closed.

We stand there for a long moment staring down at two naked lady mud flaps, a menu for the Cedarvale Grill, a collection of river stones, a handful of moose teeth, and a laminated poster of Mother Teresa.

I can read his mind.

"Quite a trip, eh?"

It was.[156]

The last miles of our family's biggest adventure ever, a shared secret among us, a permanent summer in our hearts now, where we're never apart—featured perfectly spaced rollers—the rare sort that, for a people with the right attitude and stamina, and, say, four thousand miles

---

156. Whenever things get too much to handle as a teacher, a parent, a wife, I think of those weeks spent in the wilds of Canada with the men of my life. It gets me through.

of Canada behind them, can be run like billiard balls.

Without another thought I started to run the table. My legs pumped with staccato fury, and just like that we were tucked and un-tethered, achieving a full head of steam down, the divine hand of mo-mentum back up, and a state of grace throughout, that is no less real for its being temporary and perhaps imaginary.

"We serve no hills, boys," I yelled at the approach of the next crest. "We serve no hills!"

"It's a roller coaster," Enzo howled back.

Which could be said of any of the rides, on and off the bikes, wait-ing for us back home.[157]

157. One thing we're waiting for at home is number four. We don't know yet if it's a boy or a girl but if there's a God it's a girl. Joe corrects me by saying, If there's a mer-ciful God it's a girl. Actually, I wouldn't know what to do with a girl, but whatever we have they'll be on a bike before they know it.

EDITOR'S NOTE: It's a boy!